SUCCESS
IN THE NEW
ECONOMY

Published by CelebrityPress®, Orlando, FL.

CelebrityPress® is a registered trademark.

Printed in the United States of America.

ISBN: 978-0-9991714-7-9
LCCN: 2018933571

Most CelebrityPress® titles are available at special quantity discounts for bulk purchases for sales promotions, premiums, fundraising, and educational use. Special versions or book excerpts can also be created to fit specific needs.

For more information, please write:
CelebrityPress®
520 N. Orlando Ave, #2
Winter Park, FL 32789
or call 1.877.261.4930

Visit us online at: www.CelebrityPressPublishing.com

SUCCESS IN THE NEW ECONOMY

CelebrityPress®
Winter Park, Florida

CONTENTS

CHAPTER 1

SELF-DISCIPLINE FOR SUCCESS

BY BRIAN TRACY

There is one special quality that you can develop that will guarantee you greater success, accomplishment and happiness in life. Of a thousand principles for success developed over the ages, this one quality or practice will do more to assure that you accomplish wonderful things with your life than anything else. This quality is so important that, if you don't develop it to a high degree, it is impossible for you to ever achieve what you are truly capable of achieving.

The quality that I am talking about is the quality of self-discipline. It is a habit, a practice, a philosophy and a way of living. All successful men and women are highly disciplined in the important work that they do. All unsuccessful men and women are undisciplined and unable to control their behaviors and their appetites. When you develop the same levels of high, personal discipline possessed by the most successful people in our society, you will very soon begin to achieve the same results that they do.

All great success in life is preceded by long, sustained periods of focused effort on a single goal, the most important goal, with the determination to stay with it until it is complete. Throughout history, we find that every man or woman who achieved anything lasting and worthwhile, had engaged in long, often unappreciated hours, weeks, months and even years of concentrated, disciplined work, in a particular direction. Fortunately the quality of self-discipline is something that you can learn by continuous practice, over and over, until you master it. Once you have mastered the ability to delay gratification, the ability to discipline yourself to keep your attention focused on the most important task in front of you, there is virtually no goal that you cannot accomplish and no task that you cannot complete.

Not long ago, a reporter was sent out to stand along the street in Hollywood, California. He asked people, as they went by, this one question, "How is your script coming?" Four out of five of the people passing replied quickly with the words, "Almost done!"

It is commonly known that Hollywood is full of people who have come out there hoping to write a winning movie script and sell it for a large amount of money. Many of these people work away at menial jobs for years, dreaming in the back of their mind that someday they will write a script that will sell to a major studio and solve all their problems. But the biggest problem is that they, like almost everyone else, lack the discipline to see their projects through to completion. "Almost done" usually means "never finished."

I have studied successful men and women for more than 30 years. In the simplest of terms, successful men and women are those who work almost all the time on high value tasks. Unsuccessful men and women are those who waste their time by wasting the minutes and hours of each day on low-value activities.

You see, there is a "crowding out" principle in time and personal management. It simply says that, if you spend all of your time on highly productive tasks, by the end of the day, you will have "crowded out" all the unproductive activities that might have distracted you from your real work. On the other hand, if you spend your time on low-value activities, those low-value activities will crowd out the time that you need to complete the tasks that can make all the difference in your life. And the key to this attitude toward time and personal management is always self-discipline.

There are several disciplines that you need to develop if you want to achieve your full potential. The first of these is the discipline of goals. This means that you sit down with a pad of paper, a pen and ample time. You think through and then make a written list of all the things you want to accomplish in the next one, two, three, four and five years. You organize the list into the various areas of your life; your career, your money, your family, your health and the other parts that are important to you. You set priorities among your goals and re-write your lists so that your most important goals are at the top. You then take a separate sheet of paper and you make a list of all the things that you can think of doing, right now, to move you toward the attainment of your most important goals.

Fully 97% of adult Americans are trying to live their lives without clear, specific, written goals. This is the same as setting off across an unknown country without a roadmap. You may get somewhere eventually, but it will take you much longer, and it is far more likely that you will get lost, and waste an enormous amount of time, than if you planned your trip carefully, with a roadmap, and full information about the future terrain, before you started out.

In my seminars, I ask people to make a list of ten goals they want to accomplish in the next twelve months. This simple assignment has changed the lives of many thousands of people. The simple act of writing down ten things that you want to accomplish in the next year will organize your mind and thinking at a subconscious level in ways that you cannot now understand or imagine.

Now, I meet graduates of my seminars all over the country who have performed this exercise. Almost invariably, when they opened up their lists of ten goals one year later, at least 80% of those goals had been attained, and usually, in the most remarkable ways.

So the first discipline you need to develop is the discipline of goal-setting. You should write and rewrite your goals every single day, every week, every month. If a person were to wake you up out of a sound sleep, you should know and be able to tell that person immediately what your major definite purpose in life is, at that moment.

The second discipline you need to develop for success is the discipline of planning. Many people think that they are too busy to plan. Or they don't give themselves enough time to plan. But our studies show that you will save ten minutes in execution for every minute that you invest in planning. You will get a 1000% return on your time investment by taking the time to think through, in advance, what you are going to do in the hours and days ahead.

A good friend of mine told me how he became one of the top salespeople in his industry in America. He had spun his wheels for several months when his sales manager asked him to come in on a Saturday and talk to him. This was a bit unusual, but he was frustrated with his low level of sales, so he agreed to go in on the Saturday. His sales manager then sat him down and spent the entire afternoon showing him how to plan his days, his weeks, and his months, in advance.

The very next Monday, he put these lessons into action. Within a few months he had doubled his sales. He told me that learning how to plan and budget his time, how to organize his personal resources for maximum attainment, was the turning point in his life. And, it can be the turning point in your life as well. Planning your days, weeks and months is not that complicated. You begin with a time planner of some kind. They are for sale everywhere, and in my experience, virtually any time planner you buy will help you, if you will use it on a regular basis.

You make a list of the goals you want to accomplish. Many people in sales and business make a goal of the amount they want to sell and the amount they want to earn, broken down by year, month, week, day and even by the hour.

For example, if you want to earn $50,000 per year, and you work an average of 250 days per year, this means that you want to earn $200 per day, or $25 per hour. Once you have determined that you want to earn $25 per hour, you organize every hour of every day so that you are engaged in activities that pay you $25 or more. You discipline yourself adamantly not to do anything that pays less than the $25 per hour you wish to earn.

It is amazing to me the number of people who sit around reading the paper, making their own photocopies or driving around listening to the radio who think that somehow, by some miracle, someone is going to pay them $25 per hour or more for their time. And you know exactly the kind of activities that you have to engage in that are worth $25 per hour, or more. You must discipline yourself so that for at least eight hours every day, you do only those things that pay you your desired hourly rate.

Planning begins with your making a list of everything that you have to do in the coming day, week and month. You then go through your list and you use the ABCDE method to divide your list into high and low priority tasks. An "A" task is something that is very important. There are serious consequences if you don't achieve it. People will be extremely unhappy and it can be costly to you in terms of money and success. You put an "A" next to all the activities that are vital to your success.

"B" activities are those things that you should do. These are things for which there are mild consequences if they are done or not done. The rule is that you never work on a "B" task when there is an "A" task left undone.

"C" tasks are those things that would be nice to do, but which don't really matter very much in the great scheme of things. Calling a friend, reading the paper, having a coffee break or going for lunch are "C" activities. Whether you do them or not, there will be no consequences whatever to your career.

"D" activities are those that you delegate. The rule is that you delegate everything that you possibly can to others so that you can use your precious minutes and hours each day doing only those things that are really important to your life and your career.

Sometimes people think that only managers with staffs can delegate tasks to others. But every time you buy Chinese food to take home, you are delegating the making of a meal. Each time that you have someone else wash your car or mow your lawn, you are delegating an activity. Your job is to free up as much of your time during the week for things that make a difference in your life – by delegating everything that is humanly possible to anyone else who can do it at an hourly rate lower than the hourly rate you want to earn for yourself.

The last letter in the ABCDE formula is "E" and it stands for eliminate. As you move through life, it is essential that you eliminate tasks and activities that consume a lot of time if you want to have sufficient hours in the day to do the things that are most important to you. Just as a snake sloughs off its skin every season, as you grow and mature, there are activities you need to slough off as well. There are activities that take up an enormous amount of time that you have to eliminate from your life altogether. If you don't, you will continue adding more new activities while you hold onto the old ones. Soon you will find yourself completely overwhelmed with too much to do and too little time. Eliminating low-value activities is one of the most important aspects of the discipline of planning.

The third discipline is the discipline of budgeting. This refers to both your time and your money. Every study shows that men and women who accomplish extraordinary amounts of work give an enormous amount of thought to how they use their time, and how they spend their money.

In a *Wall Street Journal* study of senior executives of Fortune 500 companies, they found that every single one of them, each of whom earned an average of $1,400,000 per year, was a systematic and continuous time planner. They gave an enormous amount of thought to how they would allocate their time on a day-to-day and hour-to-hour basis. So must you.

Whenever I speak to successful people and I ask them where they will be and what they will be doing in a couple of days or a couple of weeks, they can take out their time planners and show me exactly where they will be and how they will be using their time. When you speak to an unsuccessful person and ask him what he will be doing next Thursday, he will have no idea. For him, life is random and haphazard. Every new stop sign is an adventure. Does he turn to the right or to the left? His days just unravel like a ball of yarn rather than moving straight and true like a flying arrow toward a target.

Some people ask, "Which comes first, the tight time planning or the success?" The answer to that is quite clear. When you begin to plan your time in 10 and 15 minute blocks so that you know exactly where you will be and what you will be doing during every hour of every day, you will find yourself doing more and more things of higher and higher value. As a result, you will accomplish more and more and you will be paid increasingly higher amounts. The very act of budgeting your time or money causes you to use them both more efficiently.

The fourth discipline is the discipline of self-responsibility, the discipline of viewing yourself as being in charge of your own life.

This means seeing yourself as self-employed, as the president of your own personal services corporation.

The habit or discipline of viewing yourself as an independent contractor, selling your services to your existing company, is one of the most important paradigm shifts that has taken place in the world of work in the last 20 years. Today, all top people, no matter who signs their paycheck, and no matter what they do, view themselves as if they were totally responsible for results at their corporation. They act as if they own the place. They act as if they are the president of an entrepreneurial company with one employee, themselves, selling the highest quality and quantity of their services possible, at the best possible price.

Here is an exercise for you. Imagine that your company decided to fire everybody and hire independent contractors. You were informed that you could reapply for your job, but you would have to present a proposal outlining exactly what you would do, how much you would charge, and how the company could justify paying you these amounts. You would have to compete with other people for your job. You would have to make a complete business rationale for the amount of money that you wanted to earn by demonstrating that the company would earn far more by utilizing your services than it would end up paying you in the form of salary and benefits. Even if you own your own company, you must go through this exercise on a regular basis. It will keep you focused and highly self-responsible.

The fifth discipline is the discipline of result-orientation. Result-orientation is a hallmark of the highest performing, highest paid, most successful and most effective people in our society. They think continually in terms of the results that are expected of them rather than the activities they engage in on a day-to-day basis. They see themselves as highly productive people who have specific responsibilities to fulfill, and they never lose sight of the most important things that they can be doing.

There are five key questions that you can ask yourself, as a regular discipline, to keep yourself focused on achieving the results that are most important to you.

The first of these questions is, "What am I on the payroll?" What specifically have you been hired to accomplish? Why is it that they pay you money where you work? What is it that you contribute that entitles you to be paid as much or more than you are receiving?"

If you don't know the answer to this question with absolute clarity, make a list of everything that you feel that you have been hired to accomplish, and go through the list on your own to determine the most valuable contributions that you make. Take your list to your boss and ask your boss to organize the list in order of priority. Tell your boss that you want to be sure that you are always working on the things that he or she considers to be the most important. From that moment on, keep all of your attention focused on doing an excellent job on those few things that your boss really considers to be the highest priority.

The second question you must continually ask yourself is, "What are my highest value activities?" What are the things that you do that represent the very highest value to yourself and your company? What represents the highest pay-off? When you do these things and do them well, they really make an impact on yourself and on your organization. Once you have identified them, you must resolve to keep yourself focused on them every minute of every day.

The third question for result-orientation is, "What are my key result areas?" Many management courses are built around this concept. A "key result area" is defined as something that you are completely responsible for doing. It is specific and measurable, and it creates an output that becomes an input for someone else.

For example, if you develop a customer and make a sale, you

create business that then is fulfilled by other parts of the company. Your output is an input for other departments. What are your key result areas? What are the one or two things that you do that really make a contribution to your company? Whatever they are, dedicate yourself to doing them in an excellent fashion. Do them well, and do them before you do anything else.

The fourth question for you to ask yourself is, "What can I, and only I, do, that if done well, will make a real difference?" The answer to this question, at any given time, is only one activity. At any given time, there is only one thing that you, and only you, can do, that, if you do it really well, will make a real difference to you and your organization. It is absolutely essential that you identify this one task and then focus all your time and energy on it until it is done in an outstanding fashion. Your successful accomplishment of this key, central task can be more important to you than your completion of a whole list of other less-important activities.

The final question, and the key question in time management is, "What is the most valuable use of my time, right now?" At every minute of every day, there is an answer to this question. You must think before you begin working, and then begin working on the one thing that is more valuable to you and your company than anything else. This habit of working always on your most valuable and important tasks, lies at the heart of the entire practice of self-discipline. If you can discipline yourself to do it, there is virtually nothing that you cannot accomplish. The inability to concentrate single-mindedly on one thing, the most important thing, and stay with it until it is complete, is the number one reason for failure in life. The ability to do it is the number one reason for success.

The sixth discipline you need is the discipline of action-orientation. This requires you to develop a "sense of urgency." You develop a "fast-tempo." You continually repeat to yourself, "Do it now! Do it now!"

Action orientation is the most noticeable quality of the highest performers in every field of business and personal life. When they see something that needs to be done, they get on with it and get it done immediately. They function in "real time." They don't procrastinate or delay. They take the ball and run with it, quickly. They develop a reputation for being the kind of people that get the job done fast.

When you can combine the ability to think through your work, set specific priorities, determine your area of concentration, and then get on with it quickly, you will begin to move ahead in your life more rapidly than the other people around you.

My friend Jim Rohn says that, "Discipline weighs ounces, but regret weighs tons." Al Tomsick, the sales trainer, says that, "Success is tons of discipline."

Elbert Hubbard wrote once that, "Discipline is the ability to make yourself do what you should do, when you should do it, whether you feel like it or not."

Herbert Gray, a businessman who studied successful people for many years, concluded that successful people are simply those who make a habit of doing what unsuccessful people don't like to do. And what are these things that unsuccessful people don't like to do? Well, they turn out to be the same things that successful people don't like to do either. But successful people do them anyway because they realize that they are the price of success.

Successful people engage in activities that are goal-achieving. Unsuccessful people engage in activities that are tension-relieving. Successful people discipline themselves to have dinner before dessert. Unsuccessful people prefer to have dessert most of the time.

Successful people plan their work, and work their plan. They take the time to think through their responsibilities before they begin. They make clear decisions which they then implement immediately. They get a lot more done in a shorter period of time than the average person. And it all has to do with their disciplines. Perhaps the most important benefit of self-discipline is the personal benefit that you receive. Every act of self-discipline increases your self-esteem. It gives you a feeling of personal power and accomplishment. Each time you discipline yourself to persist in the face of distractions, diversions, and disappointments, you feel better about yourself. As you continue to discipline yourself, you achieve more and more in life.

As you achieve more things, you feel more like a winner. Your self-confidence goes up. You feel happier about yourself. You get more done and you have more energy. You earn the respect and esteem of the people around you. You get more rapid promotions and are paid more money. You live in a nicer house, drive a nicer car, and wear nicer clothes. You get a natural high from the thrill of achievement. And the more things that you achieve as the result of employing your personal habits of effectiveness and productivity, the more eager you are to achieve even higher and better tasks. Your life gets onto an upward spiral of success and happiness. You feel great about yourself most of the time.

Every act of self-discipline strengthens every other discipline in your life. Every weakness of self-discipline weakens your other disciplines as well. When you make a habit of disciplining yourself in little things, like flossing your teeth every night, you'll soon become able to discipline yourself to accomplish even larger things, like working long, long hours to bring a major task to completion.

Your entire life is an on-going battle between the forces of doing what is right and necessary on the one hand and doing what is fun and easy on the other hand. It is a battle between the forces of discipline and the forces of ease or expediency. And when you develop the strength of character that gives you complete self-mastery, self-control and self-discipline, you feel wonderful about yourself. You develop a deep inner sense of strength and confidence. You replace positive thinking with positive knowing. You reach the point inside where you absolutely know that you can do whatever it takes to achieve any goal that you can set for yourself.

Self-discipline is its own reward. Not only does it pay off in terms of greater self-esteem and a more positive mental attitude, but it pays off throughout your life in terms of the goals that you achieve and the success that you attain in everything you do.

Self-discipline is a skill and a habit that can be learned by practice. Every time you practice a little self-discipline, you become stronger and stronger. Bit by bit, you become more capable of even greater disciplines. As you become a totally self-disciplined individual, your entire future opens up in front of you like a broad highway. Everything becomes possible for you and your future becomes unlimited.

About Brian

Brian Tracy is one of the top business experts and trainers in the world. He has taught more than 5,000,000 sales people in 80 countries.

He is the President of Brian Tracy International, committed to teaching ambitious individuals how to rapidly increase their sales and personal incomes.

CHAPTER 2

WANT A MILLION-DOLLAR RETIREMENT PORTFOLIO? YOU'LL NEED A MILLION-DOLLAR ATTITUDE!

BY KARLAN TUCKER

In investing and in life, your attitude determines your altitude. Your view of money and investing determines your success as much as where you put the money. Are you patient? Are you willing to take the long view? The short view can be very volatile. By short, I'm talking 10 years.

Value investor Warren Buffet said in the *Reader's Digest* of January 2000: *"If you can't own a stock for 10 years, you shouldn't own it for 10 minutes."*

In order to wait this long, you'll need plenty of liquidity outside your stock market accounts. Historical data and recent research by Oppenheimer suggest it may require holding periods between 10 and 20 years to be certain you don't own a loss in your portfolio.

"This can be a big problem because _guaranteed monthly expenses require guaranteed monthly income_," says Darren Petty, RICP, a Denver, Colo., retirement planner. "The income must come from reliable sources – carefully selected annuities and Social Security benefits – so you can be patient and wait for the market to recover. The stock market is an efficient place to grow your money over time, but it was never intended to send you a paycheck every 30 days for 20 to 30 years in retirement."

I often remind my clients that "the purpose of money dictates where you should put it." Ask yourself, what's the purpose of your money in the market? Does the purpose warrant the risk? If yes, how much risk should you take, and on what percentage of your portfolio?

We might all think that we can be aggressive with risk when the market is rising but conservative when it's falling. In reality, we all know that the market cannot be timed! Getting out or in at all the right times to be assured of making, instead of losing money, requires omniscience. The news moves the market, and if it's in the paper, it's already in the stock price. If you attempt to time the market, you will need access to the news before others. That's called insider trading, because it does give you a distinct advantage over others – it's also illegal.

If you prefer not to lose money, then perhaps you shouldn't put it where it can be lost in the first place. You see, if your mindset and the time you're willing to wait for a gain are not realistic going into an investment, you're unlikely to achieve success.

Over the years, I've advised many people who are not comfortable buying a 10-year bank CD or a 10-year annuity because they believe it ties up their money. But putting savings in an unpredictable stock market could just as easily tie up their money! They could end up waiting 10 years just to be worth what they were the day they opened their account. In the stock market, illiquidity is always a possibility, which is why you must have a plan for guaranteed monthly income. With this plan, you can stay the course and become a better investor.

We Americans are a funny lot. We stand in line in the cold the day after Thanksgiving to get bargain prices on items we may not need. We appreciate a sale everywhere except in the stock market. There, it feels best to buy when the news is great, when everybody's making money, and as a result, prices are high. To get a deal in the market, you have to buy when the news is bad, when others are fearful and selling ownership in good businesses at deep discounts. Your point of entry (purchase) will determine your profit as much or more than when you realize them.

Warren Buffet's famous words:

> **"Be fearful when others are greedy and greedy when others are fearful."**

. . . summarize this concept very vividly.

So, what have we learned? To make money in the market, you must have resolve! The market is capable of big returns, but we may have to endure for long periods of time to make them. The point of entry into our investments is critical and often counterintuitive. Once we have made money on our bargain stocks, we have a whole new problem — how to realize our gains! To keep them, we have to sell the vehicles responsible for the gains.

Are you going to sell winners once you have won enough? If not, what's the purpose of the exercise? Markets don't only go up! Will the market be up or down the day you retire and need the money? How about the day you die and the money passes to your heirs? If it's down, will your kids wait for it to come back up before they sell? Most inheritances are spent within the first year of inheriting. A humorous bumper sticker I once saw says it best: *"Fly first class, or your kids will!"*

Secondly, you must insulate yourself from the news. Determine your long-term plan and stick with it. Perhaps the best way to do this is to not get on the Internet daily or even weekly, and don't put all your money in the market. Having safe money increases your resolve for your at-risk investments.

A now-famous fund manager found success by removing himself from the daily pressures and volatility of the stock market. He moved from New York City across the Atlantic Ocean to Zurich, Switzerland. The ocean insulated him from the fast pace on Wall Street and limited his access to the Bloomberg terminal he used for trading. The change made him a calmer and more effective money manager. He took the long view, and didn't allow short-term events to influence the long view of his holdings.

You need to buffer your emotions — watching the stock market daily plays with your emotions. It feeds greed when the market is rising and fear when it's falling. It's too easy to be too emotional about your decision-making process and make reactionary trades. Put some distance between you and the decision, some time to make a better decision. Without this policy, you may find yourself making impulsive buys or sells. Don't trade while the market is open — give yourself time to think.

Great thinking is worth more than great stock picking because even the best stocks have tremendous volatility, which pulls on your emotions.

Relying on personal experience is not always reliable. Sometimes we draw the wrong conclusion. We tend to learn better from our mistakes than from our successes. Warren Buffet says it's good to learn from our mistakes, but it's better to learn from others' mistakes. In reviewing over 5,000 portfolios in my 35-year career, I've witnessed the truth of this. I've seen what investment mistakes others have made in the past, and I've learned much from what I've seen. Their mistakes are not repeated in my portfolio or my clients' portfolios.

One common mistake is choosing an arbitrary number that our stocks and investments need to be worth (either in total or as a price per share) before selling. What if it never reaches that value? You take a bath! Or if it does get there and you're still unwilling to sell? You stay too long, and you take a bath. Why? You picked a number and anchored to it for perhaps an emotional rationale not grounded in logic and good reason.

Good thinking can't be overstated. In fact, we need to be willing to challenge our thinking on a regular basis. How did you arrive at what you believe? Was it from infallible research? When you think you're right about something, you'd better be, because from then on, you're unlikely to consider new information. Here's some good advice: *Don't believe everything you think! Keep learning.*

Perhaps you have heard it said, *"What we learn from history is that we don't learn from history."* Let's stop repeating what happened to us in 2000 and again in 2008. Almost everyone I ask tells me they lost large amounts of their portfolios, typically from 20-50%, in each of the last two market crashes. They tell themselves at the bottom that, "When I get my savings and investments restored, I'm not doing this again." Just remember that bull markets are slow and bear markets are swift. Bear markets can arrive within days or even hours, as happened on Sept. 29, 2008, when the Dow lost 400 points, which was 3.66% of its value, in **five minutes**. Then it went on to lose a total of 7% by the end of the day. The indices continued to fall, losing a total of more than 50% by March 2009.

Again on Oct. 19, 1987, the DJIA fell 22.6% in one day. If you had a million-dollar portfolio, you may have lost $226,000 in just hours. The losses totaled $500 billion market-wide that day. How could the greatest investment minds allow their clients to lose $500 billion in total within hours? It's simple, according to

John Bogle on Wall Street, nobody knows nothing (sic), which is what may have led him to start the Vanguard funds, so you didn't have to try and pick winners out of the entire herd. But even that wouldn't have prevented the losses sustained on this fateful day because the indexes, which represent the individual stocks within them, fell precipitously.

The problem with quick declines is that they may paralyze you from taking decisive action, because you already have lost more than you're comfortable with so you decide you'll stay in the market, hoping for a quick recovery, only to experience even deeper losses. One day you wake up, perhaps only weeks or months after the decline began, and find yourself down 20-50%. At that point, it likely will take years — perhaps 10 or more — just to get back to your previous high point. This roller-coaster ride can be stopped before it gets far by using trailing stop-losses. It's just not necessary to ride the market to the bottom to get all the up and then keep most of it. *If you don't have a plan for keeping it, you won't!*

Again, I stress the need for downside protection in your portfolio. Buying without a long enough time horizon or downside protection means the funds may not be there when you need them. Your timing is not the market's timing. This fact has led to the phrase, *"Buy and hold, and you may find yourself broke when you're old."*

THE ROAD TO RICHES GOES THROUGH MANY MENTAL LANDMINES

1. How am I doing compared to my neighbors, friends and peers? They often don't tell you the whole story, only the good news. How do you react to their telling of their experiences?

2. Is my spouse supportive of the decision to stay the course when the market is way down?

3. Will my kids give me a hard time over my decisions?

4. Why am I taking the risk? If you're successful, will you actually spend the newfound wealth, or will it go to the kids? Do the kids need you to be risking your retirement for them?

5. Can you be happy at the same time as when you're losing a lot of money, or will it deteriorate your quality of life?

6. If you have enough to live comfortably throughout retirement now, does it make sense to place the goose that's laying the golden eggs at risk?

People buy mutual funds in part because people are buying mutual funds. That's not a reason to own them.

The prospectus says you can lose it all, but few read it. If you read the prospectus, would you still buy?

Typically, one year after you have entered the fund, the holdings may be largely different, including up to 100% different. So, what did you buy, the holdings or the strategy? Probably the strategy, but do you know what it is? Do you know the manager behind the strategy whose decisions will make or lose you money? Do you know how long the manager has been with this fund?

The truth is, you're buying the manager more than the holdings, because as the manager, he or she will sell positions and buy new ones either slowly or rapidly as they see fit. Who is the manager? What is his or her track record?

People also buy stocks. You need to know who is the CEO of the company. How long has he or she been with the company? What is their track record? Are they throwing off excess earnings? Are they buying back stock? Are they paying dividends? How much does the CEO get paid? Do you know the answers to these questions on your stock holdings? Does your advisor? If not, get another advisor.

Warren Buffet says you should buy a company that any idiot can run because one day one will.

Your answers to the six questions above should help determine whether you should invest any money in a particular fund or stock, or even in the market as a whole. If you say yes, I want to place my earnings in the market, then the next question you need to determine is how much of your total portfolio should be considered.

There are not many people for whom the right answer is to put 100%, or anywhere near it, in the market, due to the potential emotional toll it will take on you, your relationships and your health. You need to diversify outside the market because all your holdings within the market, including your bonds, may fall at the same time. Bonds demonstrated a close correlation to stocks in the last recession, so there is no guarantee that they will act as a buffer in a declining market.

If you fell asleep and woke up 10 years later, would you have more in your portfolio than if you watched it daily?

What does this tell us about what it takes to successfully invest? Stop watching the market daily or even weekly. You can't time the market, but you can time your thinking. Become a long-term investor with only the appropriate amount of your nest egg in the market.

In summary, designing and implementing a portfolio balance is critical. Too much of your nest egg in the stock market and you may deplete your nest egg too quickly from losses and withdrawals. Not enough of your nest egg in the market and you may lose purchasing power, as the cost of living increases. A retirement income plan that optimizes the balance and timing of your portfolio is what you need, just don't wait too long to pull the trigger.

Retire happy with secure monthly income
and enjoy investing like never before.

About Karlan

Karlan Tucker has been in the financial services business for 35 years. He has personally conducted over 5,000 interviews with people nearing retirement or in retirement, helping them to live their retirements to their fullest.

He is the CEO and founder of five companies under the Tucker Financial Group Umbrella. The following companies have over $3 billion in assets under advisement.

- Tucker Advisory Group – National Insurance Marketing Organization
- Tucker Asset Management – Registered Investment Advisory firm
- Tucker Financial Services – Denver retail financial services company
- Tucker College Solutions – College coaching and funding
- Tucker Trust Realty – Investment Real Estate

Karlan Tucker is a sought-after speaker at industry events such as the Million Dollar Round Table, The Life Insurance Expo, Senior Market Advisor Expo and Insurance News Net Expo. He has personally trained more than 2,000 financial advisors and currently supports 800 advisors representing his company's products and services in 49 states. He employs 40 staff in five states that enable him to support his companies' broad offerings to their clientele.

He grew up learning the value of hard work and creative thinking on his parents' farm in Michigan. Karlan started his first business at age 16, cutting two cords of firewood daily for home consumption in his junior and senior years of high school.

Karlan then continued his education at San Diego Christian University, Harvard University, The Aileron Institute for business studies, Strategic Coach in Toronto, Canada, and The Genius Network in Phoenix, Ariz. He is a prolific reader, having read over 850 books, and currently reads one to two books weekly.

He brings a unique perspective to his clients, offering his experiences in life, business and investing. Karlan has traveled to 27 countries, and has owned businesses since he was 16 (having only worked a few times in his early life for other employers). He owns a diversified portfolio of investments and insurance products, such as life insurance, long term care and annuities, as well as precious metals and real estate, providing him firsthand experience owning most everything he recommends to his clients.

More than 10 years ago, Karlan and his wife Angela, along with close friends Mike and Lisa Redick, formed a 501(c)3 that provides community development, education and orphanages in Southeast Asia.

CHAPTER 3

HOW TO RISE UP!

BY FIKRET SUKRU

At the age of 17, my life changed forever the day I found out that my father, a 46-year-old Army Leader, was assassinated by the Iraqi government after serving the country for 25 years.

My mother put her grief aside and fought for our survival. She knew that the government would not leave us alone; everything we owned would be taken away from us and our lives would be in danger.

After a year, we decided to escape. Our escape out of Iraq was the most terrifying journey I have ever experienced. Under the cloak of darkness, my family of 13 left with a trusted guide. All we took with us were the clothes on our backs, very little money and our identification. If we were ever to be captured, we would have been assassinated on the spot.

Getting to the Iran/Iraq border was full of danger. We trekked kilometers through snowy mountains that were frequented by snipers shooting any escapees. The narrow paths were so treacherous that at one point my mother slipped. If it weren't for the quick reflexes of the hired guide, she would not be here with us today.

The physical and emotional stress took its toll. We were terrified that my young nieces and nephew would cry out and give us away. We were exhausted, but we couldn't stop. We walked on, desperate for our freedom, and slept only briefly wherever we could, including in horse stables and cemeteries.

Exhausted, cold, and hungry, we eventually made it to the refugee camp and were given a tent amongst thousands. I saw firsthand the despair, the loneliness and the fear that hung in the air. Many had missing or dead relatives. Children were weak from hunger. Every one of them had felt de-humanized and undervalued. In my mourning for my father, I came to realize that I could help those around me, and in turn, myself.

I was extremely close to my father. I would often go with him to the army barracks and I would sit for hours listening and observing. I watched how he led with strength yet treated his men and their families with kindness.

I was awed and inspired by this man whom I was proud to call my dad. While other people my age were out playing and causing mischief, I could be found sitting beside him, wearing army fatigues and a helmet far too big for me. My dad even tailored army clothes to fit me because I just wanted to be like him. Everyone has a hero and my hero was my father. And now my hero was gone.

I used all of my inner strength and leadership from my dad to change my surroundings by raising others around me. Once I started connecting with people, the word got out and within a couple of days our tent became full of people young and old. By teaching and enlightening others, I gained a lot of respect for someone so young. I gained trust from the refugee camp leader and because of this, we were able to leave the camp, go to the city and eventually escape into Turkey.

Once in Turkey, the only job I could find was delivering newspapers at 4:30 a.m. everyday. My situation changed dramatically when I began to work in a clothing store. The owner saw some potential in me and offered me a position in his importing/exporting department. I knew nothing about this industry, however, I believed in myself and I figured it out. I figured it out so well that I became a highly valuable employee and was making more money than I had ever seen.

Due to my fluency in Arabic, I was able to open new sources of revenue in the business for the owner. I started with one country and through their connections, I was able to increase our dealings to six other countries. I became so popular by building trust that people were seeking me out to export their products.

Around this time, my family decided to immigrate to Canada. For the first two years in Canada, I struggled. I didn't know any English and volunteered to gain work experience. People were constantly putting me down; including people closest to me. I refused to listen to them because I believed in my abilities and with the encouragement from my mother, I was determined to repeat my success again, so I rose above it.

I worked extremely hard, learned English and moved up the ranks to become a franchisee owner. I then made the switch to the corporate world where I moved up the ranks again to become Director of Operations in an amazing organization, as well as opening my own company. I firmly believe that my leadership and the belief in myself comes from my dad's mentoring.

From my experiences, I have based my life and successes on the following lessons I have learned:

1. Never let circumstances dictate how you feel about yourself.

I could easily have fallen into the "victim" syndrome, never pushing myself to succeed and achieve a better life for my family and myself. However, I chose to rise up.

In times of traumatic events, devastating setbacks and heartbreaking failures, our inner strength and resilience come through. Some rise to the challenge and others fall victim to the circumstance. Never let your situation (or worse, someone) dictate to you who you are as a person. Make a commitment to yourself that you have the *desire* to change and that you *will* overcome them.

One crucial lesson I learned is that you must forgive to give yourself freedom. My hurt from the loss of my father was unbearable but I knew that I could not let it destroy me. Harnessing anger, resentment and hurt will have a negative effective on your health and mind. Remember: forgiving is not a sign of weakness. It takes strength and courage to forgive and by doing so, you will release the negative effects from your life.

2. You become whom you associate with.

I loved being around my dad and watching him in action. I admired and wanted to be like him and my dad was thrilled that he could pass on what he knew to me. This molded me into the person I am today.

I have passed this onto my own son, Ali. I have always instilled in him the importance of choosing friends carefully as they have a great influence on your life. Thankfully, he has done just that by having a select group of people who are creating a life in which they should be proud of. I surround myself with amazing leaders who allow me to flourish.

Think of your friends and those you associate with at work. Do they raise you up or do they bring you down? If they raise you up and push you to succeed, then you need to keep these relationships thriving.

If not, it's time to seek a new group of people. Look for a mentor or someone you admire and go introduce yourself to them. Chances are they would be flattered and more than willing to create a mutually beneficial friendship.

3. The "Why not me?" attitude.

Attitude plays a huge part in your life. A negative attitude will affect your health, your mind, your relationships and your career. A positive one will improve your life with enormous rewards.

A lot of focus has been on the "You can do anything" attitude. I like to take it a step further by remembering something my dad told me:

*"If you see someone doing something, make
sure you do it better than they can."*

His intention was not for me to become competitive; he wanted me to believe that if someone else can do something, I can too. Just believe that you can do it better! This has stuck in my mind to this day.

Take inventory of what your strengths are. How can you use them to add value to those around you?

Ask yourself these questions:

- What are the things I am good at?
- What is it I want to achieve? …Goals? …Dreams?
- How can I contribute to my relationships/family/ friends/workplace/ community?

Perhaps the toughest question will be listing the things you are good at. They don't have to be incredible things such as "I am the world's best …." Just start small. You will find that once you start, the creativity and your confidence will begin to flow.

Next, visualize EXACTLY what you want. As a teenager, I visualized my life outside of the camp, having a wonderful life and son and how I can help others. I realized that helping others will help me rise up even more! The satisfaction in helping other people, regardless of what it is, will come back to you tenfold.

Visualizing what you want to achieve and when is a skill that will
take time to develop however, once accomplished, you will be amazed at the
results. Keep picturing that your end goal has happened already. Visualize it like a film being played before your eyes. Do not focus on HOW you will do it. If you want it badly enough, your untapped creativity will find a way.

You must see it and feel it to achieve it!

4. Help others realize their potential.

I like to see potential in others just like my father did as well as the owner of the importing/exporting company and the company I work for currently. The benefits of helping others come back to me tenfold. Far too many people expect things in return when they do someone a favour. I have found that when I inspire, uplift and encourage people to strive better, work through their challenges and help them with their passions and goals, I rise even higher than the person I am helping.

Learn to do things out of kindness for others and not expect things in return. My father would always help people and others around him who didn't understand the reasoning or the value behind it. However, he persisted in always helping others rise above their current situation, not expecting anything in return.

Developing this habit means putting aside any pre-conceived notions, judgments or stereotypes and seeing the spark that is inside everyone. Most times people are not aware of that spark so use your own unlimited talents to bring that out of them.

5. Be a "news maker" not a "news reader."

By this, I mean that it is important to make your mark wherever you go and not blend into the crowd. Make news, do not just read about someone else's news!

Wherever my dad went, people followed. What he did and said, people were eager to listen and learn. Whatever he did, he was always at the top. I have applied that same attitude in my life. The results have been incredible – both personally and professionally – and you can do it too!

Develop your own personal style of dress, the way you connect with people. Set high goals and push yourself to achieve them. Do whatever you can to stand out but make sure that you are being true to yourself without hurting and stepping on anyone. People can see through fake people very quickly and you will not get far.

*****

I have lived through some very challenging times, which thankfully, have never been repeated. All of us have a story; some are more tragic than others – but in the end, we come out stronger and we learn something about ourselves. I do not know your story. But I do know one thing: you are destined for greatness because you were given an incredible amount of untapped talent and creativity. Now is your time to rise up to meet the demands of the New Economy. Don't let your circumstances, excuses or your belief system dim your light.

Remember: be a "news maker" not a "news reader!"

To your continued success,
Fikret

About Fikret

As a visionary leader, Fikret Sukru's passion is to help individuals and businesses realize their potential and growth that they never thought possible. Fikret helps clients diminish the negative inner voice that creates barriers to prevent them from living up to their highest potential. Fikret believes that everyone has inherent gifts in order to achieve any goal they wish and his passion in life is assisting people in achieving their dreams and goals. All of his clients have experienced exponential growth in their business as well as their personal lives, and have gone on to become successful entrepreneurs and business people.

Fikret has built a progressive career in import/exporting, sales and upper management before launching his own business in 2010. Fikret has achieved his success through hard work, determination and with an unwavering passion for helping others. With over 30 years of experience in leadership roles, he knows and understands the triumphs and challenges leaders experience on a daily basis and how it can impact their business and personal life. Specializing in training and personal development, Fikret has been instrumental in the rebuilding of business practices for small business owners and large corporate clients alike. He has also partnered with many of the top motivational and leadership experts such as Bob Proctor and John C. Maxwell in order to broaden his knowledge, influence and expertise.

As a Certified Master Coach and Certified Corporate Speaker with the International Association of Corporate Speakers, Fikret regularly speaks to audiences of various sizes. His keynote speeches, full of inspiration and personal stories, speak to the hearts and minds of people to bring about immediate change and long-term results. Fikret's life story of struggle, overcoming hardships and rising to the top is truly inspirational. He uses his life experience to highlight the fact that everyone can overcome any challenge that life throws at you. So inspiring is his life story that he has been featured in various newspapers and articles.

Fikret's other passions include donating time and experience to various charitable organizations, as he firmly believes that by giving back to the community is everyone's responsibility. Perhaps his greatest passion in life is being a role model to his son, Ali.

You can connect with Fikret at:

- www.leadershipacademyinc.ca
- fsukru@leadershipacademyinc.ca
- www.twitter.com/la_academy
- http://www.facebook.com/leadershipacademyinc

CHAPTER 4

SUCCESS LESSONS: A SPORTS ANALOGY

BY J. LONGMIRE HARRISON, ESQ.

The global internet economy is transforming digital trade in all areas, including education, entrepreneurship, sports, the environment and finance. The rapid rate of change we are experiencing in the development of new communications technologies and the immense flow of ideas, technology and information will continue. Consequently, people need to engage actively in lifelong learning and must begin embracing the change in order to both understand society and remain relevant in the future. As the New Economy evolves, we must let go of old ways of thinking and doing things. To be successful in the New Economy, we will have to push our boundaries and challenge ourselves like never before.

For me, the primary "secret" to health, wealth and success in the New Economy can be stated in one concept: self-discipline. Discipline requires practice, repetition and willpower. Self–discipline is a learned behavior, the opposite of most people's natural tendencies. Having discipline is the difference between taking control of your future and life and letting your environment dictate your life and destiny.

My two formative experiences with self-discipline began when my parents told me that I had to finish my homework before I could go outside to play, and, that as long as I maintained a minimum B grade point average (GPA), I could play basketball for my school team. Anything below that and I would have to hang up my sneakers. I really wanted to play basketball, and that desire drove me to develop self-discipline. I became an honor student; President of my senior class; Vice-President of the Spanish Honor Society; Captain of the basketball team; All-State; MVP of my District 4-AAA Tournament; made the All-Star teams at invitation-only All-Star camps; received a full athletic scholarship to a NCAA Division I program – American University; and became a Captain in my senior year. I graduated from American University with a double major in International Relations and Economics with a concentration in International Trade and U.S. Foreign Policy. I represented my School of International Service at a national forum on America's Role in the Global Economy at the U.S. Air Force Academy; was awarded a one-year Japanese language and culture study abroad scholarship; and was selected as student-speaker for my university graduation. I went on to play professional basketball in Japan, and later became an attorney.

I believe having self-discipline served me well in the past and has served me well both in my professional career as an attorney, and as a parent of a daughter with special needs. It will also serve me well as I step into the future and embark on a new journey involving the digital transformation impacting our world.

While self-discipline is key, there are other factors that also contribute to success, both in life and in the New Economy. As a former athlete, I draw many life lessons from sports, and believe sports have a lot to teach us about discipline, success, and adaptability. To learn and earn in the New Economy, individuals and companies should develop the mindset of a professional athlete and continually improve their 21st Century digital media skills. Below are some key characteristics for success:

1. **Top Traits of Successful Athletes**

There are several common features and traits that successful athletes share. Most likely you already have some of these traits, and even if you don't, you can develop them with practice and perseverance.

- **They Are Fearless** – Well ... no one is completely fearless, but successful athletes, and successful individuals, push through boundaries. They feel the fear and then have enough confidence in their convictions to work through the fear and meet the challenge.

- **They Make Actionable Game Plans** – Making plans and setting goals is an important step to success. Just as athletic teams have game plans, we also need strategies for success in life. But at some point, after making plans the next step has to become taking action to execute the plan.

- **They Adapt to Change** – Athletes on pro teams sometimes get traded or injured, and must adapt to new circumstances. In the New Economy, every business that exists today will not be here tomorrow. Think about the technologies from the past that are now obsolete, for example. Keep your eye on the future and adapt.

- **They Play the Game** – Just showing up is a start, but, it's not enough. You have to play. To get your desired outcome, know that you will sweat, exert maximum energy at times and ride waves of emotional ups and downs. But standing in victory makes it all worth it.

- **They Spend Energy Efficiently** – Are you just running up and down the court? Or are you working effectively and producing? If you're not spending your energy efficiently, you won't win the game, you'll just be exhausted with no stats to show for your work.

2. <u>Game Performance Reflects Preparation</u>

Any professional athlete will tell you that you're only as good as your preparation. If you don't practice hard, you can't play hard. And if you don't play hard, you won't win. The effort you are willing to dedicate to the background work of your business will determine how far you will go. Serena Williams, LeBron James, Kobe Bryant, Alex Rodriguez, and other elite athletes all know that the hours you put in off the field determine how far you go on the field. To be a success in the New Economy, you have to be willing to:

- **Practice** – Do dry-runs of your processes to make sure they work.

- **Listen to Your Coach** – Accept feedback from your mentors and coaches without getting defensive. They're just trying to make you the best you can be.

- **Try New Things** – Adjust your grip on the club, try a new marketing angle, take a few risks in a practice game to see how it works.

- **Work with Your Teammates** – Team spirit is built in the hours on the practice field, in the dugout, and in the locker room between games. What can you do to create a spirit of teamwork?

3. <u>Building Skills to Reach Success</u>

Just as athletes practice and expand their games during the off season, in order to build your skills and reach toward success, you'll need to push your boundaries and improve your game. You can start slow, or you can dive right in, but these tips will help you move past your fears quickly and gain experience feeling success.

- **Become the Expert and/or have a Specialization** – The more you do to develop your expertise, the more confidence you'll have, the more successful you'll become, and the more value you'll add.

- **Continuous Improvement and Learning** – If you devote just one hour a day to learning something new, then move on to something else when you've mastered it, you'll be able to maintain and expand your skills.

- **Keep Abreast of Industry News** – Take some time every day to read up on current trends and events in your industry. You can set up news or terms dashboards that are important in your field to stay aware of what is happening at all times.

4. Mindset and Mental Toughness: Thoughts and Actions That Block Success

Successful athletes must be mentally tough – they have to stay in the moment and not let previous mistakes or missed opportunities replay in their minds. Likewise, your thoughts play a huge role in whether or not you'll experience success or failure. Some thoughts can cloud success or cause you to downplay your successes instead of celebrating them. Mental issues that can block success are:

- **Having Impostor Syndrome** – This is a condition that many people share. No matter how much success and kudos they achieve, they still feel like a fraud or undeserving. Realize that you're uniquely qualified for what you do and learn to accept that.

- **Comparing Yourself to Others** – There's no need to be just like your competition. In fact, one reason you study your competition is to learn how to distinguish yourself. You're a unique person with your own way of doing things and this is what makes you great.

- **Being Preoccupied with What Others Think** – If you spend all your time thinking about what everyone around you is thinking, you'll never be able to be truly successful. Instead of thinking about what others think, consider what you think. Can you look in the mirror every day and be proud of your actions? That's what's important.

- **Overthinking Every Situation** – It's good to look at situations from every angle, but once you do that you should be able to make a decision. Overthinking stems from a fear of failure. While it's not a bad thing in and of itself to worry about failure, if you're too afraid of failure you may end up procrastinating on your decision, which can make it worse. Trust your instincts. Once the game begins, trust in your preparation.

- **Believing That Perfection Exists** – One of the biggest mental roadblocks is thinking perfection exists. This can cause procrastination and indecisiveness. Don't let perfect become the enemy of good. Sometimes we need to accept that good is good enough. You can always improve later. In sports, designed plays often don't work out exactly as planned, but are effective enough to result in a score.

- **Life Events** - Sometimes life gets in the way and your motivation may suffer. When emergencies and family issues arise, take care of them. But don't ever give up on attaining your goals. Instead, handle the situation, then refocus on your goals once the situation is under control.

To overcome these success blockers, you first have to acknowledge that you may do them from time to time. For example, if you have often called yourself a perfectionist, take a hard look at yourself and you might find that you're not a perfectionist at all, you're just scared to be wrong and to fail. Let that go and move forward so you can put some success under your belt. The more you know how that feels, the more you'll want to experience it.

Success is no secret and...

Success is no accident. It is hard work, perseverance,

learning, studying, sacrifice and most of all, love of

what you are doing or learning to do.

~ Pele

...5, ...4, ...the final ticks of the clock are flickering, ...certain plays from the game flash through your mind, ...3, ...the path you had to take to get you here, in this moment, the good times, the bad times, the injuries and setbacks, the bounce backs and getting back to your feet, the relationships lost and found, the sacrifices made, ...2, ...these are the final seconds, ...1, ...did you coast through or have you played all out? Are you at peace and proud of how you played?

The key to success is in your hands. It is up to you to be the successful person you've always dreamed of. I wish you luck and all the best. I'd love to hear from you and learn about your motivational success or challenges. Please feel free to contact me to access the PDFs referenced in this chapter and make use of the software and online tools designed to help you stay organized, focused and motivated.

To your success – and to a winning season!

About J. Longmire

J. Longmire Harrison, Esq. lives in the Washington, D.C. area with his wife and daughter. He is from the mountains of Asheville, N.C., and has a passion for education, sports, travel, languages and life.

J. Longmire is fluent in Japanese, and for the past 10 years has worked as a Japanese litigation consultant on cases involving global price-fixing, market share allocation, bid-rigging, mergers & acquisitions, foreign corrupt practices and other matters involving international trade. Previously, he practiced as a foreign legal consultant in Japan. He also served as liaison for the nation's first U.S. – Japan Environmental Technology Initiative in conjunction with the White House Council on Environmental Quality's Interagency Environmental Technology Office and the Global Environmental Technology Foundation.

Prior to his legal career, J. Longmire worked in Japan for Toyota Motor Corporation in a dual role, both as a member of Toyota's International Public Affairs, Government & Industrial Relations Group, and as a professional ball player for Toyota's basketball team in the top division of the Japan Basketball League (JBL). After leaving Toyota, J. Longmire founded The Future All-Stars Society (The FASS), where he developed and managed educational, cultural and basketball exchanges between Japan and the U.S. involving the New York Knicks, with operations in Washington, DC, New York, and Delaware. He also represented sports agents and JBL teams in recruiting and placing American players in the JBL. In addition, he conducted basketball and English language camps in Japan.

J. Longmire earned his Juris Doctor from Howard University School of Law and an LLM in International Environmental Law from George Washington University School of Law. He received a Bachelor of Arts degree from American University in Washington, D.C. with a double major in International Relations and Economics, and a concentration in International Trade and U.S. Foreign Policy . He also studied at Reitaku University in Japan where he graduated with a Certificate of Japanese Language and Culture.

J. Longmire is now using his legal and entrepreneurial experience to create media platforms that address 21st Century digital media skills and digital trade involving environmental issues, education, sports, and entrepreneurship.

You can connect with J. Longmire at:

- http://jlongmire.com
- https://linkedin.com/in/jlongmireharrison
- https://facebook.com/jlongmireharrison
- https://instagram.com/jlongmireharrison
- https://twitter.com/jlongmire01

CHAPTER 5

WHY BRANDING IS A MUST FOR SUCCESS IN TODAY'S ECONOMY

BY KIMBERLY P. TAYLOR

If you're a business owner, you have undoubtedly noticed that competition today is fiercer than ever. That said, how you set your business apart is critical to your success. In this chapter, we will discuss how creating a brand for your company is a must for enjoying success in today's economy.

So, what exactly is "branding"? According to Merriam-Webster, the noun "branding" means "the promoting of a product or service by identifying it with a particular brand." In other words, branding is the process of establishing your company's identity, as well as visually creating a message that quickly explains what your company does or the services it offers. Good branding represents the total summation of a company's reputation, and even a customer's perception of the level of customer service they can expect (think Ritz-Carlton, a brand that consistently delivers exceptional customer service). In addition, good branding can provide employees with motivation, direction, and a clear vision of your company's mission statement. A great brand can truly be a point of inspiration around which your entire team can rally.

Like me, you may be surprised to learn that many small-to-medium-sized businesses are still not convinced of the importance of building a strong brand. A lack of passion for one's personal or business brand continually perplexes me. Do they just want to remain a "mom and pop shop" or do they want to grow? Don't get me wrong. It's okay with me if a "mom and pop shop" wishes to stay local and serve locals. But they still need an identifiable brand. For businesses that have the potential to have a regional or national reach, do they understand the value of creating an identifiable brand that their customers will be drawn to and will make the continual effort to repeat business with them?

Many national brands have been born from a local or regional brand that gets adopted quickly by the consumer and/or is propelled into the economy by major economic players (e.g., *Shark Tank*, venture capitalists, or private investors). When considering your business offerings, are they local, regional, national, or international? No matter the level of exposure, your brand should stand the test of time.

For now, let's talk more in depth about branding and what it should look and feel like. Branding could include the creation of an icon – also referred to as a logo – (think Target, Best Buy, Harley-Davidson or Chick-fil-A), or branding could simply entail typesetting the lettering of the business name to establish a company's look and feel (think Google, Chobani, Humana or FedEx). Clearly, it's understandable why a national or international company would want to have a well-established logo/brand. But if it's that important for the big guys, why would it not also be as important for the small mom and pop shops or medium-size businesses as well? After all, establishing a strong brand at a local level may one-day lead that business to having a regional, national, or even an international reach.

To my point, let me share a real-life example of an experience I had a few years back with some great guys I worked with in Houston, whom I still admire to this day. I and an associate at the time, were charged with the task of taking a father/son surgeon team from a small, three-exam room office and moving them across town to a completely different hospital system all within a matter of a few short months. In addition to moving them across town, part of the job entailed designing and building out an 8,000-square foot, state-of-the-art private surgical practice with eight exam rooms, a procedure room, two registered dietitian offices, a psychologist's office, classroom areas, business and billing offices, three surgeon offices, and a retail storefront all within the footprint of a new office space. In addition, I strongly encouraged them to create a new brand identity even though they had been known by a specific business name for well over 30 years.

In addition to moving them and designing and building out a new clinic, it was also my task to create the new brand name, design a logo, file their DBA with the county clerk, and begin creating all the assets required to launch a new marketing campaign simultaneously with the opening of the new clinic. The new assets included a new logo, new website, new billboards, new out-of-home campaign, a new print campaign, and radio.

So, what exactly did I do and what was the outcome? Here is the case study I put together that really gives a great overview of how I took a local business, branded them, and crafted an international brand from scratch:

Case Study #1: Crafting an International Brand in the Heart of Houston | THE DAVIS CLINIC

Problem:

Houston Surgical Consultants featured renowned bariatric surgeons who had landed a reality show on the TLC network called *Big Medicine*. To their surprise, they were not equipped to handle the subsequent calls and new patient inquiries in their tiny, three-exam room office in the Texas Medical Center.

Action:

I was recruited to aid in the re-engineering of an innovative weight-loss surgery and weight management clinic, and I helped build it into a five-star rating for a truly comprehensive bariatric program. I worked as an onsite consultant, acting in the role of Marketing & Administrative Director, where I directed administrative, financial and daily operations of a three-surgeon clinic, handled all aspects of marketing, advertising, and public relations, and managed all non-clinical/administrative staff. In addition, I was the key point person related to their relocation from The Methodist Hospital in the Texas Medical Center to Memorial Hermann Memorial City Hospital's campus. There, I helped to design and build out an 8,000-square foot, state-of-the-art clinic. We re-staffed, re-trained, and re-focused the practice to be customer service oriented, with the emphasis on patients being our customers. We continued shooting a final season for TLC's *Big Medicine*, and re-runs of the show ran in over 33 countries around the world.

Result:

Prior to the new clinic's opening, I worked to develop a new logo, filed a new DBA for the practice with the county clerk, and developed a comprehensive, multi-layered marketing campaign that would launch simultaneously in support of the new clinic opening. Here is a glimpse of the results that followed:

- Developed and managed new patient intake processes, resulting in a 59% increase of net revenues over a 4.5-year period
- Grew business positive cash flow from starting A/R of $400,000 monthly to $1.8M monthly
- Decreased A/R from 120+ days to 45 days
- Overall case volume increased from ~300 cases annually to ~850 annually
- We saw new patients come from all around the globe from places such as Egypt, Saudi Arabia, Dubai, Mexico, Brazil, Canada, and England

As you can see, the project was a great success, and while it initially took some convincing, the surgeons understood that to move forward, progress, and build their dream, it required them to let go of "the old" and embrace "the new". Ultimately, the surgeons were able to recruit a third surgeon and almost triple the number of surgeries they were able to provide to patients. They were also able to sell their practice to a larger physician group, allowing the father of the original duo to retire.

Here is another case study showing how I established another healthcare brand in major metropolitan cities across the U.S.A. As you will see, this marketing effort also yielded tremendous results. There is something to be said for branding and the power it can yield in growing business:

<u>Case Study #2:</u> A Case Study for JourneyLite BARIATRIC PARTNERS, INC.

Problem:

JourneyLite was a fast-growing network of specialized outpatient surgical facilities providing the Laparoscopic Adjustable Gastric Band, also known as the LAP-BAND® System. Although successful upon opening its first center, senior management did not feel that the branding or advertising aspects of their initial campaign properly supported the level of professionalism or quality they were establishing in their center programs.

Action:

After working to develop JourneyLite's new brand identity, I worked to create a national multimedia campaign that would launch in seven different U.S. markets and support the new branding and marketing objectives. The campaign needed to be broad enough to support the brand over all possible forms of media. The campaign's objective was to increase the number of weight loss seminar sign-ups via the JourneyLite website and to increase phone registrations. A secondary objective was to secure

JourneyLite's position as the market leader in the laparoscopic LAP-BAND procedure. The campaign sought to reinforce the positive, life-changing results that the LAP-BAND system could have for people considering weight loss surgery, and to demonstrate the quality and professionalism of the JourneyLite physicians and staff.

After selecting an agency to work with, I pulled a team together to do initial research. In addition, I had conversations with prominent JourneyLite surgeons, senior management, and patients. My team embarked on an ambitious marketing campaign with the new look and feel of the JourneyLite brand. It was clear that, for many people who have struggled with their weight, the archetypal "thin and beautiful" models represented unrealistic weight loss goals. JourneyLite was about making lifestyle changes, not just cosmetic changes, so real-life patients were featured in the campaign. Some were shown early in their weight loss journey and others closer to the end.

I worked with my team to execute a layered campaign, alternating media strategies to keep JourneyLite as top-of-mind. Different media was used in different markets to maximize the marketing budget. Calls-to-action were changed for the appropriate market as needed. For the campaign, we created newspaper and magazine ads, outdoor billboards, web banner ads, out-of-home boards, direct mail pieces, and radio spots. I rewrote and revamped the entire JourneyLite website and worked with SEO/SEM experts to perform search engine marketing and optimization work to propel JourneyLite into the top tier of LAP-BAND and weight loss surgery keyword search results.

In keeping with the new brand, the headlines and body copy were insightful, relevant, and spoke directly to the target in an upbeat and meaningful manner. To connect JourneyLite to the LAP-BAND brand, each deliverable included the benefits of the LAP-BAND procedure, mention of the experienced surgeon partners, and the JourneyLite logo and tagline. In some markets where the surgeons already had a brand presence, individual surgeons were featured in small space, B&W ads to leverage their brand identity. Each deliverable had a clear call to action and directed potential candidates to register for a free seminar, either through the JourneyLite website or via the call center.

Result:

- One month after we launched the new campaign in the Houston market, JourneyLite saw a 58% increase in website traffic, referrals, and seminar registrations
- In the Los Angeles market, there was a 127% overall increase in seminar attendance in the three months immediately following the new campaign launch
- These upward trends continued, and two months after the launch, JourneyLite had a record-breaking week, with seminar registrations up an additional 30% from the previous record
- Campaign generated over $1.5M in the first six months of initial launch

In the above case study, again you can see how good branding and consistent use of the brand within an advertising campaign produced great results.

SUMMARY

To recap, branding – when done correctly – should provide the following for your business:

1. Improved Recognition
2. Advertising Support
3. A Sense of Trust with Customers
4. Financial Value
5. New Customer Lead Generation and Conversion
6. Employee Buy-In of your Vision and Mission Statement

The most successful and profitable companies have one thing in common, a solid brand. They have set themselves apart as industry leaders through the process of building a strong brand. Building a strong brand does not happen overnight, but it can happen with time, investment, and consistent use.

If you're a small to medium-size business that has not yet established a solid brand, now is the time to do so. What are you waiting for? Branding your business is a must for success in today's economy.

About Kimberly P. Taylor

Kimberly P. Taylor founded Taylor & Associates, LLC in February 2008 and rebranded her company to Taylor Marketing Works in January of 2015. She relocated from Houston, Texas, in 2017 to the greater San Antonio, Texas, area where she serves her clients in the beautiful Texas Hill Country. Kimberly has over 25 years' solid, hands-on experience in marketing and public relations strategies and implementation, strategic planning, brand identity, business development, advertising, and trade show and event management. In addition, approximately ten years of her career was spent in radio and TV broadcast production. She specializes in business-to-consumer marketing, with an emphasis on new customer acquisitions.

Prior to forming Taylor Marketing Works, Kimberly served as Director of Marketing & Brand Strategy for Bariatric Partners, Inc., headquartered in Charlotte, North Carolina, where she marketed outpatient surgery centers in cities across the country under the brand name "JourneyLite". Before joining Bariatric Partners, Inc., she was the Director of Marketing & Business Development for University General Hospital Systems, LLP in Houston, Texas. In addition, she established the first bariatric program for the Memorial Hermann Healthcare System in Houston, Texas, where she ran a highly successful comprehensive program for several years.

With a passion for making a difference in the lives of the morbidly obese, Kimberly has served as a National Advisory Board Member for the ASMBS Foundation and is a Past-National Vice-Chair for the ASMBS Foundation's *Walk from Obesity*[SM]. She is an Editorial Advisory Board Member of *WLS Lifestyles* magazine, and her ongoing column, "Observations from an Obesity ~~Survivor~~ Overcomer," appeared for several years in the magazine quarterly across the nation. She has presented at the Annual ASMBS Conference and has served as an adjunct faculty member for BariMD as a resource to clients seeking expertise in bariatric marketing. She has served as a consultant to Ethicon Endo-Surgery, a division of Johnson & Johnson, helping to create their online bariatric patient portal by writing much of the content. In addition, she has presented at the American Marketing Association (Houston Healthcare) and her creative work placed as a semi-finalist for the American Marketing Association Houston Chapter's Crystal Awards.

Kimberly was responsible for coordinating the shooting schedule with the cast and crew of TLC's *BIG MEDICINE* and worked for almost five years with Drs. Garth and Robert Davis, to create and implement The Davis Clinic, *the* premier comprehensive weight management program in the State of Texas. Additional past and present clients include Symbion Healthcare (Nashville, TN), BariMD (Ft. Lauderdale, FL), rdSolutions (Houston, TX), Triangle Chiropractic (Austin, TX), Camille Cash, MD (Houston, TX), Bailey Surgical Assistants, LLC (Houston, TX), Silver Fox Management Company, LLC (Houston, TX), Kathryn Lanigan Pruitt, JD (Dallas, TX), Cowboy Steak House (Kerrville, TX), Solbrig Hearing Center (Kerrville, TX), Ken Stoepel Ford-Lincoln (Kerrville, TX), OutBack Patio Furnishings (Marble Falls/ Kerrville, TX), The Ranch Radio Group (Fredericksburg, TX), Hill Country Telephone Cooperative/HCTC (Ingram, TX), Holloway Plumbing (Kerrville, TX), and Guadalupe Bank (Kerrville, Ingram, Fredericksburg, TX).

When Kimberly isn't working, she enjoys spending time with her husband and daughter, and exploring the beautiful Texas Hill Country.

Contact information for Kimberly:

- Email: Kimberly.Taylor@TaylorMarketingWorks.com
- Website: www.taylormarketingworks.com

CHAPTER 6

SUCCESS IN HEALTH IN THE NEW ECONOMY

BY HENRY J. "TRIP" GOOLSBY, MD

You will resemble, tomorrow, the dominating thoughts that you keep in your mind today!
~ Napoleon Hill, *The Law of Success*

Joan is a fifty-six-year-old mid-level executive who came to me seeking help for multiple medical problems. She was extensively evaluated over the preceding six years by several other health care providers.

These providers diagnosed her with various maladies, including Lupus, rheumatoid arthritis, Crohn's disease, ulcerative colitis, fibromyalgia, irritable bowel, adult onset diabetes mellitus, degenerative arthritis, hypothyroidism, sleep apnea, anxiety, depression, and multiple blood lipid abnormalities.

At the age of 32, Joan underwent a complete hysterectomy and subsequently was advised to discontinue all hormone therapies because of the "potential risk" of cancer and heart disease. Additionally, she was prescribed numerous pharmaceuticals by these physicians in the attempt to control the symptoms of her "diseases." Joan decided that she had had enough when, after a cursory exam, a review of recent laboratories, the abbreviated discussion and then prescription of yet a third medication attempting to regulate her glucose metabolism by her primary internist.

By the time Joan came to see me, she was at her wits end and fed up with all the prescription medications she was taking. And, even though she was an avid road-biking enthusiast, she remained frustrated by her persistent mild obesity.

After I ran a complete female metabolic and hormone laboratory profile, her results indicated multiple suboptimal hormone levels, suboptimal metabolite levels, and evidence of ongoing liver damage.

Accordingly, I designed a comprehensive precision treatment program to address these challenges to her health. This program included lifestyle (nutrition and exercise) programs, transformational motivational mindfulness (empowered medicine) training, in conjunction with bio-identical hormone replacement therapy and metabolic optimization. Eventually, I introduced biofeedback training to her in an effort to enhance her stress threshold parameters, as this stress was also having an adverse impact on her multiple chronic disease processes.

Week six through eight of her program were greeted with a significant lowering of her blood sugar levels, as well as removal of all anti-anxiety and antidepressant medications. Joan began to feel a significantly increased sense of well-being and calm, with improved sleep habits and near complete resolution of her "fibromyalgia" and "irritable bowel/colitis" symptoms.

Her liver function tests significantly improved, and her hemoglobin A1c dropped from 9.2 to 7.0 (a normal A1c level range is 4.8 to 5.6). On the fourth month of follow-up, her liver tests were normal and her A1c was out of diabetic range at 5.9— after having stopped all medications for her diabetes about six weeks earlier. Joan is bicycling avidly and expects to complete her first century ride in the near future, her average speed having increased from 12 mph to 15.6 mph on her last 20-mile outing.

After reviewing these significant improvements, the big question was, how did Joan accomplish the near complete resolution of her diabetes, her metabolic syndrome, her steatohepatitis, her depression and gastrointestinal syndrome, as well as her fibromyalgia and arthritic complaints, in only five short months?

Joan would be quick to respond that the creation of a successful health image and the empowering motivational mindfulness exercises facilitated the constructive thoughts and decisions that energized her successful outcomes. She would then say her physician helped her a little too.

Over the past fifty years, the accomplishments of medical science have evolved dramatically. A poignant example would be the progression from the somewhat irregular responses of a particular malignant tumor type following the administration of crude chemotherapy medications, to the perfect arrest of cancer growth in a patient diffusely encumbered with the same disease by administration of precision-targeted biologicals.

Reconciling the advances of the basic sciences with the complexities of clinical application and methodology to this day challenge the most sophisticated research academician. A reason for this challenge resides in the foundations of clinical medical research, which are still subject to the vagaries of pre-quantum mathematical calculations.

These calculations give rise to the placebo effect, and occur because the observer, whoever that may be, is assumed to exercise no influence on the outcome of the research. Anyone who has participated in, chaired, or enrolled individuals in clinical trials work is intimately familiar with the fallacy of this thought (the "observers" potentially being the source of significant "influence," regardless of attempted randomization and placebo distribution). These observer effects are commonly known as the Hawthorne effect and the observer-expectancy effect.

Natural science does not simply describe and explain nature; it is part of the interplay between nature and ourselves.
~ Werner Heisenberg; Nobel Laureate Physics

We are only beginning to appreciate the profound effects we may achieve through the practical application of our intent, desire, and belief to the image of our successful health. So impressive are the anecdotes of health recovery from multiple and significant illness, that the implementation of a motivational mindfulness – empowered medicine – approach should always be included as a facet of therapy, so as to enhance and ultimately achieve the successful image of health.

We **are** capable of having the health we desire. And many of us have, for the most part, enjoyed many years unencumbered by significant illness and/or disease. This period of grace, if you will, relied more or less on the following two conditions:

1) The genetic gifts of our parents to us (our genome), and
2) The abuse we subject this genome to, via internal and external stressors.

When we exhaust most or all of our reserves, we develop symptoms and signs of disease, but this is not the end. Even at the point where "dis"ease becomes apparent, we may recover a significant degree, if not all, of our health by successfully committing to a program of empowered recovery.

Many of us do just this when we receive the wake-up call that our shrinking reserve provides (annoying symptoms that prevent us from avidly participating as we once were accustomed). This opportunity, the emergence of our turning point, allows us to change direction and pursue a path directed to a more desirable outcome (better health).

We are born with incredible resilience and flexibility when it comes to recovering from injury and insults of many types. The plasticity of the different organ systems to recovery is inborn and always ready to respond—and recover from—even the most catastrophic events. Each of us has the potential for seemingly endless improvement from virtually any aspect of our lives. This ability is a natural process that is defined and contained in our genetic infrastructure and how we utilize it. Understanding the nature of this self- empowering gift gives us a robust ability to succeed at any convalescent recovery (or any other endeavor) we so choose.

The empowerment process abides by natural, universal guidelines that, once brought to our conscious level of understanding, allow us to apply them to achieve our best results. Many of us use any number, or all of these universal laws, instinctively. Most of us, however, have never been exposed to the concept of these laws, nor how we might become attuned, aware and benefit from our conscious intention to achieve, and subsequent subconscious implementation of our intent to acquire and/or maintain awesome health.

> *Accidents, old age, (disease) and death itself come from*
> *holding wrong mental pictures. When a man sees himself*
> *as God sees him, he will become a radiant being,*
> *timeless, birthless, and deathless.*
> ~ Florence Shinn, *Your Word Is Your Wand* (1928)

The principles here are fairly straightforward and easy to apply once understood. They have, to date, secured the vision and motivated thousands of individuals to achieve their empowered successful health image and beyond. Being dynamic and continuous in nature, they invariably compensate the user by allowing perspectives on ever-improved health images when the existing image of success has been attained. Let's use Joan's success as our example.

It is clear Joan knew what she *did not* want – continued waning health. Her turning point was reached during that visit when she was offered more medications despite her continuing health deterioration and the accompanying ambiguous future outcome. Additionally, her "Medical Mastermind," (the healthcare team allied for the single-minded purpose of creating a successful health outcome for its creator) was not harmoniously aligned with her expressed healthcare goals (resolution of the disease states causing the problems). Finding the knowledgeable, compassionate, sympathetic, like-minded team members to facilitate her success was the first and critical step to its realization. This infrastructure is available to us all as we seek to create our empowered health. No compromise should be accepted in its acquisition.

The most important factor in achieving Joan's successful health image was its creation. Knowing the dynamic nature of the empowered successful health image was important for Joan. At the outset of our collaboration, her previous experience constrained her thoughts and beliefs, limiting the ultimate vision of success. Many of these limiting convictions were reviewed and progressively altered over the course of her multiple subsequent victories (e.g., she guffawed at the initial thought of an average speed of 15 mph on her bicycle). An important challenge for Joan was reconciling the existence of her health outcome based on the appearance of the desire. The appearance of these goals for us all is the sign we may achieve them and their pre-existence. Belief is the operant action in this setting as it motivates and influences our vision into the final outcome. It did for Joan, as she began to see success after success related to her image she progressively empowered her outcomes and replaced her limiting beliefs with increasing motivation, desire and focused intent.

Empowered outcomes are those that dwell in the individual's ability to provide the power of intent to well-founded informatics that define the optimum characteristics of (recovered) health. The actions taken to arrive at the end result in Joan's case were those related to her lifestyle efforts. Her exercise and nutritional intake modifications that were accomplished with thoughtful guidance by her "Mastermind" are being well compensated by the interim laboratory parameters showing her metabolic syndrome has resolved. I fully anticipate completed resolution of her diabetes on her upcoming blood work. It was a pleasure to see active gratitude for her anticipated gains reflected regularly in a journal she kept to chronicle her progress.

In many ways, Joan intuitively displayed a keen ability with the natural universal laws. This was demonstrated by her capability of accepting the initial status of her health without complaint and focusing on her successful health image. In reality, she simultaneously accepted and forgave herself for her creative role in the development of her poor health. At that moment she actually acknowledged her grateful ability to become aware of her role and of the newfound ability to create a significantly improved lifetime outcome. More importantly, contrary to choosing a stressful, obstructive, pugilistic response to her medical condition, Joan conceptualized her initial poor health as an opportunity, empowering a response of intent, resolve, peace and creativity.

As with many patients, significant lifestyle changes are charged with the challenges of sacrifice and acquisition of novel thought processes and actions that mature into new lifestyle habits. Joan was no stranger to the occasional setback or deviation, particularly those of old nutritional vices (dietary carbohydrate content). She did however, finally realize the compelling truth that for every advance or improvement in her health character she must ultimately choose to sacrifice a less desirable character or habit.

Every gain of virtue necessitates some loss in vice; every accession of holiness means some selfish pleasure yielded up; and every forward step on the path of Truth demands the forfeit of some self-assertive error.
~ James Allen

Lastly, Joan developed, by virtue of her intellectual and contemplative efforts, a highly compliant attitude that permitted intuitive and practiced adherence to these natural universal laws.

These laws are at work for every decision, thought, and action we may take—whether we are conscious of it or not. By their understanding and habitual use, we take charge of the elements of success in our lives and thus become empowered creators of our health and not simply the demoralized victims of randomness.

The thought (Infinite Law of Thinking) and expectation (Infinite Law of Supply and Infinite Law of Attraction) of extraordinary health and well-being will give rise to just that with adherence (Infinite Law of Receiving and Infinite Law of Increase) to the image created. Ultimately, the health we obtain (Infinite Law of Compensation) in the setting of this newfound obedient behavior (Infinite Law of Forgiveness) will replace the issues created (Infinite Law of Sacrifice) by our historically-disobedient behaviors. And by consistent application of the laws, our new behaviors allow (Infinite Law of Nonresistance) the laws to work to our benefits.

###

About "Trip" Goolsby, MD

Henry J. "Trip" Goolsby, MD is Board Certified in Internal Medicine and Medical Oncology, and is a Certified Elite Health/Longevity Medicine provider. For over thirty years, Dr. Trip has been setting the bar and leading the way in providing patient-centric healthcare. And, he continues to do so by being the forerunner in bringing a whole body, mind and soul approach to healthcare services in Louisiana via Infinite Health Integrative Medicine Center.

Presently, patients from all over the globe seek Dr. Trip out for his expertise in precision integrative health optimization, longevity and regenerative medicine. His approach to motivational and transformational mindfulness medicine empowers his patient-partners every day, enabling them to transcend limited perceptions of what is possible for their health. His progressive motivational approach transcends, not just health, but also lives.

For more information about Dr. Trip, visit:

- www.YourInfiniteHealth.com

CHAPTER 7

BECOME AN ENTREPRENEUR IN THE NEW ECONOMY

BY TAMEKA DYON

Radical shifts. That is what we've experienced in this transition to a new economy. Powered by a rise in technological advances, innovative platforms, and grassroots organizations, our individual entrepreneurial voices have grown stronger and louder. Perpetual resilience in many business arenas seem to be achievable for anyone that works smart, and because of that, nearly everyone is becoming an entrepreneur in some sense of the word.

Think about it: How many people do you know that *only* work one 9-5, with no means of extra income? If they don't get extra income from anywhere, what are they saying about their finances? How many people do you know with a hobby that they've monetized, a side job, a hustle, or whatever else you want to call it? According to CNN, more than 44 million people have a side hustle[1]. More and more, this new economy has given us the ability to decide the important: what we want to do to achieve the level of success we desire.

---

1. http://money.cnn.com/2017/07/12/pf/side-hustle/index.html

A COMMUNITY ECONOMY

How did we get to this community economy where entrepreneurs owning small businesses began to thrive? A few years ago, you may recall hearing words like recession, down-sizing, and restructuring. These words were the fuel that seemed to construct the ground floor of where we are today. People were getting laid off from jobs that they had once thought they would retire from. In the last five years, roughly one-fifth of all U.S. workers[2] have been laid off. That number does not sound like much, until you consider the number of people living in the U.S. Because of that, I believe that we were forced to this place. Company loyalty went out of the window. Retirements were questionable. People did what they needed to do to get to the next level of their lives. With growing changes in technology, it has become easier for businesses to create, to produce, and to touch customers from all over the world. Thus, radical and massive shifts are being made in the realm of entrepreneurship creating a sweet spot that everyone can take advantage of.

We've known for years that entrepreneurs were willing to take on more risk than normal to achieve success, but now we have new views on the role of "thought leaders." Those new expectations arrive with titles like intrapreneurs, where executives are charged with the task of cultivating and advancing innovative ideas that will help with competitive advantage and change the world-type theories. You see, even employers encourage entrepreneurship in some form. We have solopreneurs, those that run their companies from A to Z, doing everything themselves so that they can minimize their costs and expenses while maximizing returns or maybe put to use skill sets that they were unable to use before. We cannot forget the sidepreneurs, those that run and operate their businesses along with a full-time job. This makes up many of the individuals that I've encountered along my journey as an entrepreneur. No matter which way you classify yourself, most of

2. http://www.latimes.com/business/la-fi-layoffs-unemployment-jobs-economy-20140924-story.html

us have the same goals: to pursue sustainability in our businesses, to gain social mobility, and to secure financial prosperity.

This new economy is the best time to break free from coloring inside the lines and truly foster that entrepreneurial mindset. Here are four key pointers that startups can use to succeed in the new economy:

1. **Use a Grassroots Approach**

   It's no secret that grassroots organizations are created to inspire positive changes that influence economic movement. I'm not talking about fads or trends, but instead true change in the communities in which we live and work in today. The most successful organizations are those that speak to the core of community filled with people working together for a common goal.

   With any business, you must find a resolution to a problem that many people face. If you are offering products or services, taking a grassroots approach to your offerings can be very helpful. No matter what your organization offers, there is most likely a community of individuals that will be its primary audience. Partner with that community to garner input and feedback as you move throughout the development phase. Do your research, make assessments, and deploy resolutions that respond to the community's need. Start small and create an organization that people can stand beside.

2. **Find Your Niche**

   Hopefully you are not in business just to make a quick buck. If you are, then you are in for a surprise. If you focus on the impact, positive change, and problem resolution, you should eventually see a return on your investment.

   Select a niche, drilling down to the most basic level of offering that you can. Remember that you cannot be everything for everybody; that is what leads so many people down the road to disaster. Focus on one thing and solve one problem at a time. Start small and master your niche. Eventually your small business will grow out to solve bigger problems for a much wider audience. Amazon, Google, and Apple, just to name a few, are companies that started small and grew far beyond what we could have all imagined.

3. Make Use of Technology

The distance in which the advances in technology have traveled is simply jaw dropping. Technology has served entrepreneurs well in this new age through providing a clear and easy path to the communities that need us most. Visibility, access, and capability are the three major factors that technology provides.

Social media is a driving force in the business world. It's the easiest and most cost-effective method of increased visibility. Companies like Facebook[3] did not exist a century ago, but now host over two million active users monthly. These companies have also revolutionized the way we connect with our audience.

4. Pivot! Pivot! Pivot!

Everything you put your hands on is not always going to succeed. Being able to identify areas that need change are paramount to the success of your business. A pivot takes place once you recognize that something isn't working in your business and needs to change. I can't stress enough the importance of recognizing the need to pivot, but more often than not, entrepreneurs struggle with recognizing the need for change. In this new economy, change is invaluable. Recognizing trends, staying abreast of important data, and understanding every aspect of supply and demand as it relates to your industry is vital. The ability to spot bumps in the road and adjust accordingly are traits that are highly valued.

3. https://newsroom.fb.com/company-info/

SUMMARY

The new economy has done a great job at proving that local grassroots alternatives can be successful combining innovative ideas from around the country to build a significant community-based economy. As entrepreneurs, take advantage of the opportunity that this new economical atmosphere allows:

1. Act with a grassroots mindset.
2. Find Your Niche.
3. Make use of technology.
4. Remember to pivot.

About Tameka

Tameka Dyon helps her clients share their stories with people all over the world. As a four- time author, Tameka specializes in working with nonfiction writers that desire to become published authors. Tameka began writing in 1987 and at the young age of twelve, her first poem was published. Tameka understands the power of written words and launched a publishing company to help people educate and inform.

Tameka's publishing career is centered on her philosophy that "sharing your knowledge can change a life." Her goal is to help her clients share the knowledge they have gained through experience and education with their readers. She believes that every entrepreneur should write a book to further solidify their standing as an expert in their industry. Tameka also built a program that teaches individuals that would like to write a book, but may be unsure of where to start, what they can do to successfully achieve that goal.

She helps her clients share their personal stories and triumphs as well as their successful business advice. Tameka's clientele is diverse – ranging from college students that want to educate high schoolers on tips to a great freshman year to an entrepreneur with a million-dollar business that wants to educate people on how to duplicate her success.

Tameka is a graduate of Mississippi University for Women. She is the CEO of Impact Learning Publications, a publishing company specializing in writing services and publishing of nonfiction books. Tameka is also a best-selling author. She has been featured in the *Huffington Post, BuzzFeed*, and other media outlets. Tameka has also spoken professionally at conferences in several states – diving into writing, publishing, empowerment, and entrepreneurship related topics.

You can connect with Tameka at:

- www.ilpublications.com

CHAPTER 8

HOW TO START A BUSINESS IN THE NEW ECONOMY

BY DR. LESA ANSELL

Success is defined differently by different people. To me, success means doing what I love every day. To others it may be achieving a certain financial level, owning a certain house, or time freedom. But how do you become successful? First you have to define what "success" means to you. After that, you simply research the necessary steps, formulate a plan, and execute the plan. That's easy, right? Well, as the saying goes, if it was easy, everyone would do it. So, how did I get there?

When I was young, I was told to find something I love, and to figure out how to make money at it, and you will never work a day in your life. I thought, "Wow! That is definitely what I want!" The problem for me was I loved many things. I still do. So, one of my biggest pitfalls was to streamline all of the things I like into a career. That is where my struggle really began. I developed two competing careers. I had colleagues on both sides of the street that did not understand how I could do both careers. These were medicine (as a nurse at the time) and chiropractic.

Medicine believes that health comes from the outside in (i.e., taking medicine) and chiropractic believes that health comes from the inside out (i.e., correcting the nerve interference caused by subluxation of the spine). But, I believed to be healthy many of us needed to blend both approaches. But, how do you do that when these two entities are in stark contrast to each other? I decided I did not have to live with the construct that either created, and I set forth to learn everything I could about both. Then I earned the degrees necessary to blend both worlds, while preserving my autonomy that was essential for my happiness and success.

In doing that, I took what appears to be the long, hard road. However, when you love the process of learning as much as I do, that is part of the fun of the journey. I earned my nurse practitioner degree, and then my certifications as a laser professional, and certification as a medical aesthetics injector. Finally, I had found the formula to do what I love every day (success), make money at it (survival), and never "work" again a day in my life (happiness). This led me to opening a med spa where I get to focus on wellness (chiropractic), follow patients medically (nurse practitioner) and in general, just help people to feel better, look better, and be better.

Honestly, the opening of a business is the easy part. I know first-hand because it is the third practice I have opened. One was a partnership; one was a corporation, and the current one is a sole proprietorship. The day-to-day decisions, financial planning and backing, and business plan, are the true keys to driving a business forward to success. The biggest pitfall I see in new start-ups is lack of business planning and lack of funding. Before I opened my first partnership practice, we raised the capital needed and secured additional funding. We researched the best prices for the equipment we would need and determined if it was more cost-effective to purchase it outright or to fund it. We had a plan and we stuck to it closely. Eventually, it was time to dissolve the partnership and part ways. Fortunately, there was a plan in place for that as well.

The next venture stemmed from the need to serve my patients, but be independent from the previous practice. Again, I did research. Again, I raised capital. This time though, I felt vulnerable. I was alone, and unprotected. So, after speaking to my CPA, I decided that it was best to be under the protection of a corporation. This venture lasted until the opportunity presented itself to merge with another practice that was medical and thereby gave me the opportunity to learn new skills, and acquire more knowledge that would serve my future patients/clients even more. However, a few more lessons were awaiting me. Some of which I could have prevented by a little more negotiation in my contract, and others which could not.

This brings me to the final practice. This time, I took the knowledge and skills I learned, performed more research, raised more capital, and followed my heart. I knew that I needed and wanted a change. I found the thing that I was most passionate about, gained more skill, earned more certifications, and opened the type of practice I had only dared to dream of. I drew from past experience, reached out to my previous patient base, and examined previous lessons learned to glean what was positive that I could keep, and what didn't work that I should avoid.

Through this process, over 20 years, one thing was certain. I had to keep "reinventing myself" to stay relevant and on-top of my game. But how could I do that? With every change, I looked at the marketplace to determine what the consumer was looking for. I looked at the standards for my industry(s). Then I set out to not meet them, but exceed them in service and integrity. Being impeccable in your word will build a strong reputation of trust. And the truth is people refer to people they know, they like, and they trust.

But how do you build this reputation? How do you gather your followers, your tribe, as Seth Godin calls them? I have found many ways that are successful for this. The first thing I did was to join the Chamber of Commerce. I had to get to know the connectors—the people who know the people. Next, volunteer where your heart leads you. Do it just "because," not for a specific gain, but to pay it forward. When people see that you are genuine, and care about your community, they will like and trust you, which will eventually turn to referrals. Join networking groups. The main one I chose was BNI (Business Network International). In this group, they only allow one person per field of experience, so you will be the only "expert" in your area of expertise.

And finally, do everything you can on social media to build a positive reputation. But do it well, and do it right. Be honest. Be interesting. Be relevant. Do not just put sales-type information on your sites. People want to feel as though they know you. Again, they refer to who they "know," like, and trust. This particular piece of reputation-building was difficult for me. I had no idea which platforms to use. I didn't know the "rules" for certain media sites. I learned the hard way for one, by getting a direct statement to me about "being too wordy." Due to that, I started to research more so I would get the best use out of the sites using the algorithms that they use to determine post/ad success.

With the new social media world, anything you did ten years ago in marketing, and perhaps even in the day-to-day business, is likely irrelevant. The landscape in the social media world is constantly evolving and therefore, so are the algorithms, which can make you successful, or bury your ad. It is essential to hire the right people who are knowledgeable in this area and have the time to dedicate to this. They will also be the individuals who will take care of all of your digital marketing. They will help you build a successful website, create your ad words, help you attain top status in searches so more people see your ads or website, and even perform a "check-in" campaign to keep your Facebook status in front of people.

However, even if you do all of that right, you still may not be successful if you miss the mark on other key items, like customer service, integrity, and value. Things like keeping your promises, returning calls, following up on items left open, etc., are essential for trust, as is to "under-sell," and "over-deliver." And of course, there is no substitute for good old-fashioned hard work. You have to have the "all-in" mindset and commitment to your business or product. This is the thing that keeps driving you on days that you might want to quit. In the end, your effort and commitment will overcome any risks you took in starting your business venture and the reward will be a prosperous, successful business.

Another key to success in business is diversity. The more you can offer your patrons, clients, or even patients, the more likely they will return for additional goods or services. In my business, a med spa, we offer four different laser therapies, Botox and fillers, Bioidentical hormone replacement, chiropractic care, massage, infrared sauna treatment, traditional medical care, pain management, and medical weight loss programs. We also offer products and supplements from manufacturers we trust. Because of changing our business structure, we were able to cross-market services throughout our patient/client base and cross-sell when a new patient/client came in. Often, when a patient comes in for chiropractic, they become a client on the med spa side, and vice versa.

If you create legendary experiences for your customers, they will not want to go anywhere else. By offering a variety of services by the same friendly staff, they already know the level of service they will receive when trying something new. These memorable experiences create word-of-mouth marketing that is both free and truly invaluable. When you create these type relationships with patients/clients, they will stay, pay, and refer! In addition, when one of them comes to you to support their cause, or their child's fundraiser, honor the commitment they made to you and support them. This will only strengthen the good will between you and them.

In everything you do, you must have an ability to market your skills. You should have a small "elevator speech" to tell people succinctly what you do and why. Try not to monopolize the conversation, and always return the kindness by showing interest in what they do as well. You might just find that you have businesses that complement each other, and do not compete, and therefore can become a cross-referral source. The more people you know, the more likely the chance of finding great business relationships. So, get out of your business, so that you can work on your business. Meet the people who know the things you need to know, and surround yourself with successful people who know more, or different things, than you do. Research can help with this as well.

Whenever you do research, you want to make sure that you manage the information appropriately. Only use what is valuable to you. Not everyone has the same needs. When looking at success, first YOU have to define what that is for you. Every industry is different, so not all information or strategies will fit all businesses. You must also have the discipline to manage your business properly (regulations, laws, etc.), so that you can hold onto the business. You want to strive for success but plan for failure. That means having an exit strategy. But in addition, ensure you have enough capital to carry you through until you become profitable. For some businesses, that could take years.

Doing a projection before you open can help you have realistic expectations, and not fall into the trap of undercapitalization. By utilizing the services of attorneys (for contracts and business structure) and the small business association, you can properly plan the business and get started the right way. And my final advice is to be passionate in your daily endeavors. People like to surround themselves with happy people who are successful. Be that bright light that others are attracted to. It will definitely spark your success.

About Dr. Lesa

Dr. Ansell is a multidisciplinary provider who specializes in chiropractic, aesthetic medicine, allopathic medicine, and functional medicine. She has attained a unique skill set and immense training to provide a unique approach to people's health and beauty concerns. She describes herself as being in the "solutions business."

In her career as a nurse, which started at age 15, she has received certifications and licensure as a certified nursing assistant, licensed practical nurse, registered nurse (ADN, BSN, and MSN), and then became a nurse practitioner specializing in Adult and Geriatric Care. She then moved her focus to aesthetics and pain management. She attained her certification in Cosmetic Injections (Botox and Fillers course) and then earned four certifications in Laser Therapy to become a laser professional. In addition, she trained as a Legal Nurse Consultant and paramedic.

She is a licensed Doctor of Chiropractic. She continues to expand this career by continuing to learn new techniques and therapies to benefit her patients. She had the opportunity to introduce chiropractic to a Pain Management practice, where in turn, due to her status as a nurse practitioner, she was able to gain additional training and skill in pain management injections to include Supartz injections for chronic knee pain, steroid injections for shoulder pain, trigger point injections and Botox for headaches, which complimented her experience as a Certified Injector. She also received training in bioidentical hormone replacement, and performs pellet injection therapy in her practice. Dr. Ansell has also been a nursing instructor and continues to teach the National Council Licensing Exam (NCLEX) Nursing Board Review. Her teaching experience also includes teaching CPR for over 30 years, teaching in the Chiropractic Program, and private tutoring for nursing students. She aspires to open her own Laser Therapy Program to help others attain certification to begin an exciting career that they can tailor around their family's needs.

When Dr. Ansell is not working in her med spa, she can be found at Mission Arlington Medical Clinic, where she works as a nurse practitioner and chiropractor. She began there as a student, and volunteered chiropractic care. Upon graduation, she continued to volunteer there until eventually joining the staff. She is one of the team doctors for the NPSFL Dallas Defenders Football team and has traveled with the team since its inception. She is an examiner for the National Board of Chiropractic Examiners, and also serves as the Chief Nursing Officer/Supervisory Nurse Specialist for the Disaster Medical Assistance Team, TX 4 DMAT. In this position, she leads the medical care during national disasters, such as hurricanes, in the mobile hospitals that the team sets up and staffs during these disasters.

She has earned degrees from Oklahoma State University, the University of Texas, Maryville University, and Parker University. She plans to start the Doctorate of Nursing Practice program in the Fall of 2018. She has authored the book, *Alternatives in Health Care*, which she wrote as a guide for patients to use when trying to determine which path of care is best for them.

You can connect with Dr. Ansell at:

- resolutionsmedspa@outlook.com
- www.resolutions214.com
- www.twitter.com/ReSolutions214@Solutions214
- www.facebook.com/ReSolutionsMedSpa-ProadjusterChiropractic@ Dr.Ansell

CHAPTER 9

YOU'VE GOT WHAT IT TAKES

BY BLESSING AYEMHERE

Success is who you are and not what you have.

Many people define themselves by what they have, the social status attained, influential people they know, and the wealth they have accumulated (in the amount of cash in the bank or by the amount of real estate they possess). Some even pride themselves in the number of businesses established; the environment and societal pressure have contributed to this in no small way, but that does not change the fact that measuring success by what you have is an illusion. This is because, what you have can grow wings and fly away. There are records galore in history of people who once abounded in these things, but later discovered the futility of acquiring them without focusing on who they are becoming or have become; who you are remains fundamental to the lasting things in life you can achieve and attract.

Please don't get me wrong, acquiring and possessing these highlighted beautiful things of life is fantastic, but the emphasis here is that those things must not be what define you, but what you do with those things you have justly and genuinely acquired, in life. Who you are and what you do with the opportunities and privileges that come your way, is what attracts its material equivalent in the ecosystem. For me, it's about the legacy, the memorial and impact you have made or can make in life. I recognized this early in my life and career and decided to focus on improving who I am and can be. I had to stop focusing on what I had or didn't have and started focusing on what I wanted to be and how I could get there. I am still a work in progress, but looking back, I am grateful to God for the privileges and opportunities He has given me to recognize early in life that I can deliberately alter who I am and can be.

I learnt early in life to pay less attention to how people will feel or how the environment regards what I had to do to add value to my life, as long as I was within the boundaries of legality, morality and civility. I stoop to do things that the average young man out there will not do because of what people may say or the societal perception. You know what? People will always have an opinion no matter what you do, and opinion is one thing that is common to everyone no matter the class or social status. If you are worried about what people will say if you do what you need to do to pay your bills, train yourself or your children or start a business, you may have to also worry about what they will say when you eventually are unable to pay those bills or get thrown out of the house because of unpaid bills.

For myself, I had to take up work at building and construction sites to generate funds to pay for my education and tuition. This was one of the many not too complimentary things I had to do to ensure that who I am is enhanced for both personal benefit and public appeal. You must work on increasing your value, otherwise the New Economy may not recognize and give you your true worth and value. One man I respect very well, Myles Munroe of Blessed Memory, once said that life does not give you what you deserve but what you negotiate. The New Economy is a global village where convergence and engagement are on an international scale. It's an ecosystem that rewards the daring; it does not recognize tribe, colour, region or geographical affiliation.

If you can engage the ecosystem enough to produce solutions for the needs of people, the New Economy places you in the league of achievers. It's a disruptive era and only imagination works not limitation.

To succeed in the New Economy, you must identify challenges and needs around you and figure out the resultant impact of such challenges and difficulties on people around you. The emergence of UBER, Airbnb, Proville.net lends credence to this fact. While it continues to be important to satisfy customer's needs, the New Economy requires that you look inwards and figure out the challenges you are going through and imagine what relief solving that problem will bring to you. That might be a pointer to the possible relief people going through the same challenge may have when they get their problem solved. These are exactly the things I am doing today.

I have learnt how to use Leverage. Leverage is a term used in financial parlance to describe the relationship between an owner's equity and a borrowed fund. A borrowed fund here can be likened to using what does not primarily belong to you to achieve what you want – with due permission and authorization. When you use the term in finance, it means in very simple terms, that you have some funds (Equity or Shareholder's fund) but it's not enough, so you borrow to add and make up what is required. In reality, we all have some form of equity that can be added to, if we are careful enough to look inwardly, discover and deploy the resources at our disposal.

HOW I LEVERAGE RESOURCES

1. I have learnt a few things in life that work for me, I see these things as my equity that I can add to improve the lives of people. So, what I have done is to create the InspireXtra Empowerment Initiatives (I-Xtra). I discovered that lots of people are struggling to break free from the limitations placed on them from their background, either due to

parental, economical or societal constraint. Some people feel they could have done better if only they had all the right parental support, were sent to school or sponsored in business. While having these basics as rights that every child should be given, we must accept the fact that many are being denied them. So, looking around and seeing people who are making progress because they are educated whilst all you do is feel bad and/or bitter, won't change anything. As simple as this statement is, it's startling how many people have condemned themselves to regret and animosity. They are resentful to their parents (even when their parents are no more); they blame society for being unfair to them and all the other negatives.

At i-Xtra, we decided to leverage the information and access that we have to people. I discovered that knowledge and information had saved me, so I gather people together in small businesses and informational meetings for men called "LEVERAGE" and what we do is to share information about trends and innovations and how we can deploy them in business and problem solving. We also leverage on the networks of people we have who come to us, like the TEDx show, where experts in their own rights come to help us build capacity and open our eyes to trends and possibilities, and the outcome has been phenomenal. Annually, we organize an event called the "Greatness! Possibility!" Conference. This is usually an exceptional business and leadership conference, with about a thousand participants at our last event. The excitement of ensuring that people don't have to be subjected to what I suffered, and the fact that I am using my hard-earned income to improve the lives of people is simply exhilarating.

Initially, along with the challenge of starting this as my concept, was the problem of how I could fund it – given that my intention was not to charge for my training and seminars. The reason for not charging is simply because most of the people I want to reach out to, might not be able to afford payment for seminar(s). In fact, I am fully aware of the fact that not many people want to spend money for personal development. It is those who know and value knowledge enough who will pay to acquire it.

So, since my focus is to equip people with this knowledge and bridge the information gap, I have to ensure I went the extra mile. I spend huge sums on training and personal development around the world just to be able to share this knowledge with these wonderful people for free. The reason behind this endeavor is the fact that I am what I am today because of the knowledge gained and the information available to me hitherto. So, if everyone can acquire good knowledge and become informed, there is a great possibility they will do better things with their lives. I love to see people transition from the defeatist mentality to the abundance mindset, because that is exactly what I am currently enjoying.

2. I have also learnt to leverage for commercial value. I know the knowledge at my disposal can be commercialized as well if only I look carefully enough. Hence, the incorporation of Proville.net – a platform that bridges the gap between service providers and service buyers.

This idea did not originate from me; it is an idea that already existed in some parts of the world. So, for me, leveraging is also about looking for what is trending elsewhere and creatively domesticating it to bring in the cultural uniqueness required to make it work in your chosen ecosystem. Today, Proville.net is solving problems for people who no longer have to leave their homes in search of professionals that can offer services to them. This is how the New Economy works. The world is global in nature with everything at our fingertips, people seek convenience and if you offer that, your relevance in the New Economy is guaranteed.

You must learn to innovate in this dispensation; it's all about genuine value addition and problem solving. You must identify what is not working and ask yourself, can this work? Can I make it work? How will making this work improve the lives of people? *Voilà!* You are on your way to becoming relevant in the scheme of things. There has never been a better time to be alive than now. It's a season of endless possibilities, but only for those that can deliberately and consciously look for it. You must enlist yourself today, be creative with what is around you or what you think ought to be around you, but only exists in other regions of the world. It all starts with the passion to see yourself as a problem solver rather than one of those looking for things that are not working to complain about.

The interesting thing is if your goal is to look for sympathizers, you will get more than enough; people who are going nowhere, people who will help you magnify the problems around you and tell you why things cannot change. I strongly advise that you focus on what is working around and outside your immediate environment, and leverage on those things. It's a known fact that our environment affects how we rise or fall; it shapes our culture and influences our view of the world. However, it's not every environmental factor that is outside our control. Research has categorized environmental analysis into the internal and external, the controllable and uncontrollable.

While the influence of the external environment may be outside of our immediate control - things like government policies, economics, legalities, culture or technological change, we must learn to use the barriers as enablers. And do you know why? Because most people are facing the same difficulty imposed by the environment. However, we must be conscious of the environmental factors that lie within our control – things like our attitude to life, our character and disposition to risk and willingness to engage fledgling opportunities. We must cultivate an "I can do" mindset if we plan to be among the influencers of this world.

You have what it takes to create your own economy, to redefine your world and to become a person of influence. This must start from within you, your value system and your ability to delay gratification. You must learn to respect times and seasons, find an inner peace and be content per time.

About Blessing

Blessing Obehi Ayemhere believes that everyone has greatness on the inside. As one who has defied culture and environmental limitations, Blessing's commitment is to inspire, mentor and coach people to greatness and unlimited possibilities. We strongly believe that the average youths have in them creative ideas, gifts and potentials for greatness which, if put to use, would be of great benefit not only to them but to the nation and the world as a whole. We believe that when people are empowered with the right information and other useful resources, there would be positive results, and when inspired to break their limits and boundaries and effect innovation and productivity in their lives and businesses, there would be better leadership and more positive impacts.

Blessing O. Ayemhere, is the President of Inspirextra Empowerment Initiative and a certified High Performance Coach from the High Performance Institute, California, USA. He has more than 20 years of experience in the corporate world where he has executed different high level and executive jobs including strategic planning, financial strategy, credit, loan and risk syndication (including business startups and expansions). Blessing is passionate about teaching, coaching and supporting business startup initiatives with relevant information and link-bridging.

Blessing is a highly sought-after teacher, speaker, business and leadership consultant. He is the convener of the Greatness Possibility conference; an exceptional gathering of people who are desirous of attaining greater heights in business, family achievement, career, finance and wellness. He is also the convener of LEVERAGE (a men's business forum).

Blessing Ayemhere is a graduate of Banking and Finance from the University of Benin, Benin City. He also holds an MBA in International Business Management (Lagos) and an M.Sc. in Strategic Planning from the Edinburgh Business School, Heriot Watt University, Scotland, and UK. He has attended executive training programs at Stanford University and Harvard University in the USA, and holds a Leadership certification from IESE Business School, Barcelona, Spain. Blessing Ayemhere is a Graduate of the Chief Executive Programme (CEP) and an Alumnus of the Lagos Business School. He is a Fellow of the Institute of Chartered Accountants of Nigeria (FCA) and a Fellow of the Chartered Institute of Taxation of Nigeria (FCTI).

Blessing, who started his career as an audit trainee with Spiropoulos & Co. (now Grant Thornton International) in Nigeria in 1997, rose within the ranks to audit manager. He had a stint in the financial industry thereafter before joining the Oil & Gas sector and is currently a senior executive.

You can connect at:

- blessing.ayemhere@ixtraog.com
- twitter: @blessed_oba;   @ixtraog

CHAPTER 10

"LIFE, LIBERTY AND THE PURSUIT . . . "

BY GARY D. WHITE

Thomas Jefferson first penned these words back in 1776 – words which would find themselves forever imbedded in not only the Declaration of Independence, but also as memorable lines for generations to come. I wonder if much thought was given to the impact these few written words would have on mankind.

In the original draft, Jefferson included the word *"happiness"* as a right granted to every human, both present and in the future, by their Creator. As you might imagine, there was quite a bit of debate as to the intent or definition of the word "happiness" as all these words were to be included in the most significant document of its time. Since being a property owner was tremendously important at this time in history, the word was thought to have its intent tied to landownership, with a narrower meaning towards prosperity or one's wellbeing. But, as with everything else, happiness in its simplest terms is defined not by Thomas Jefferson, history or Mr. Webster, but by whomever happens to be discussing the subject at the time. The definition becomes their idea, their belief and their perception, and it may or may not be in line with your definition.

Growing up in a small town in the Panhandle of Florida, my

father was the Chief Deputy of the county Sheriff's Department and later went on to serve as the Executive Director and Chief Investigator for the State of Florida in their 14th Judicial Circuit. He spent 38 of his 63 short life years in law enforcement, serving the people in that great state. My father never graduated high school, having quit school during the 8th grade. He never attended college but received his education about life from life. He did, however, return several years later and received his GED, an accomplishment he was most proud of.

I learned the better part of my life lessons from my late father. He was then, and is still today, a great source of inspiration and wisdom for me. One such tid-bit he shared with me was this:

Everybody knows what to do with the bull,
except for the man that's got him by the horns.

Now at this point you may be asking yourself what does bull wrangling and words from the Declaration of Independence have to do with Success? Simply this: Success is defined not by books, videos, CD's or the latest and greatest motivational speaker, but by the one who is *'holding on'* whilst in pursuit of it.

In his first team meeting as head coach of the Green Bay Packers in 1959, Coach Vince Lombardi shared these words of wisdom with his team:

Gentlemen, we shall chase perfection, and we will chase it relentlessly. Knowing all the while we can never attain it. But along the way, we shall catch excellence. I'm not remotely interested in just being good.

If any coach in the history of football could be classified or defined as a success, he'd be at the top of the ladder. But contained in those words I read, I believe he knew success or perfection was going to be three (3) things:

1. On-going.
2. A pursuit, something to be sought after.
3. Never fully reached.

Now before you start throwing your hands up and quitting because you too feel like success is something that only *"other people"* achieve, consider this: I believe Coach Lombardi himself equated perfection as the ultimate success, one that NO ONE ever achieves, but still MUST be pursued. The "excellence" he mentions that shall be caught is made up of the moments, the victories and losses along the way that ARE within everyone's reach along their life's journey.

The New York Mets was one of baseball's first expansion teams, they were founded in 1962 to replace the Brooklyn Dodgers and the New York Giants. Their first season earned them the unfortunate title: "The worst team in baseball history." A record that stands true even today (just don't remind a Met's fan of this distinction). The team was comprised of players that probably should have already retired or entered into the coaching profession. Yet, even as bad as they were, they still managed to win 1/3 of their games. You know why? They showed up when it was game time.

During that same time period, the New York Yankees were just beginning their baseball dynasty. The team was comprised of future Hall of Famers such as Whitey Ford, Yogi Berra, Mickey Mantle and Roger Maris. They finished first in the American League, won the World Series against the Cincinnati Reds, but yet they still managed to lose 1/3 of their games. Why, you ask? Because the other team showed up. The moral of the story being: In life, no matter how good you are at whatever you choose to do, you're still going to lose 1/3 of your *"games."* No matter how bad you may feel you are at your profession, you're still going to win 1/3 of your *"games"* just by showing up ready to play. It's in the other 1/3 that we need to concentrate on being our best. This is where we can, and should, make a difference in the pursuit of success.

After spending several years in law enforcement myself, working in patrol, narcotics, undercover and homicide, looking back I recall that it was during the pursuit (chasing the bad guy or gal), that I found the most excitement and fun. Don't get me wrong, putting the 'cuffs' on someone who you believe has committed a crime and hauling them off to jail is rewarding. But there is no more fun (legally) than the pursuit of the bad guy.

Stop for a moment and consider what I'm trying to get across to you in this short time we have together, and the point is that Success is:
- Something that most everyone is trying to achieve in life.
- Everyone has a different opinion of what success actually is or isn't.
- Requires varying degrees of time to acquire it.

Now, I'm going to ask you to consider what I feel is THE most important element for success. In your personal search for whatever success in life you seek, enjoy the pursuit!

Bill Gates (who I think we'd all agree is a successful person, at least in business), shared these words of wisdom regarding success:

Success is a lousy teacher in life. It seduces smart people into believing that they can't lose.

My personal take on his quote is simply that on my journey towards obtaining success, I'm going to win some and I'm going to lose some. If I personally choose to become successful, then why not enjoy the pursuit on the way to reaching my success? Think back for a moment to one of your proudest accomplishments and consider no matter how long it took you to reach your goal (your success), even if there were bumps, pot holes, and crazy drivers along the journey, without the pursuit, reaching your goal would be far less sweet and memorable without it.

If you search history, you will find that as long as there have been men, there have been stories to tell. Some men are better story tellers than others, but most love to tell stories. As a matter of fact, the greatest man to ever walk this planet was also the greatest story teller of all time. He used stories to get His point across in a relatable fashion. One of the best things about stories is that, like good wine, they get better with age, or at least they get bigger. Take a moment to recall the last time you heard a story from a friend, co-worker or family member. If they were trying to purchase a new car from a dealership, I'd wager the storyteller focused more on the pursuit (the negotiations, the back-and-forth with the salesman or manager and the haggling), and how difficult it may have been, more than they did on actually receiving their new car.

Speaking of stories, a friend of mine – who I'll call Rob – shared with me that back in the 80's (anyone remember them?), he was an Executive VP for a large corporation, with offices in London, Paris, California, and New York. He shared with me that, at the time, his income level was well into six figures and he considered himself quite successful. One day, he received an offer from another company which was quite attractive. Among a long list of perks was included a potential ownership stake in the company that would be available in the near future, and so he accepted the offer.

Unfortunately, within just a few short weeks after accepting the new position, he soon learned that the business was in serious financial peril and would probably be closing within 12 to 14 months. His hopes and dreams of being part of something much larger than himself, his opportunity to fulfill a life-long dream of owning his own business, all of those things were rapidly slipping through his fingers and there was nothing he could do to stop it.

At the new company, he was charged with the responsibility of managing the final development of a new product. His first thoughts were to "abandon ship!" But he told me that the challenge of the new product was intriguing enough that he decided to stick it out while looking for employment elsewhere. Over the next 12 months, he not only developed the new product, but he learned it inside out. Unfortunately, shortly thereafter the business did in fact fail and closed its doors.

But there's a Cinderella story ending to this tragic tale. As Rob was sharing his all-too-real story with me, he suddenly related how that by forcing himself to make the most of a bad situation, and learning the new product backwards and forward, this allowed him to start his own company which sustained him and his family for the next two years and eventually allowed him to go into the ministry full-time—where he remains today. Now I don't want to take away from the story's end (the success), but can you see how the success wouldn't have been possible without the pursuit?

I see young men and ladies fresh out of college desperately wanting to be catapulted immediately into the Penthouse suite or the corner office with CEO or President emblazoned on their office door, and I think what a tragedy it would be to deprive them of their own pursuit – which myself and others have endured, suffered through and enjoyed in pursuit of our own successes.

To them, along with other countrymen both near and far, I say... "Slow down, take your time and enjoy every step of your pursuit. Today's moments will soon become tomorrow's memories."

If Thomas Jefferson were here today, I believe I'd walk right up and ask him to tell me stories not of his successes, but of his relentless pursuits in achieving them.

Godspeed!

About Gary

Gary White is a Market Sales Trainer with SCI Corporation (Dignity Memorial), coaching and training new sales executives in the Dallas/Ft. Worth marketplace. Coaching, mentoring and training others is Gary's true calling and passion. He states, "Helping others find their true calling in life and then providing the guidance and training to help them become content with their journey to success is what makes it worth it for me."

Gary holds an MBA in Business Administration from the Provident University of Delaware.

After spending nearly a decade working with the State of Florida as a Homicide Investigator, Gary entered the private sector as a sales associate with AFLAC and excelled in sales and marketing – serving as a District, Regional Sales Coordinator and a State Sales Trainer in Alabama and Florida. Gary has landed coverage in print and broadcast outlets in the *Success Today Show, Wall Street Journal* and *USA Today.* In addition to his extensive sales and marketing experience, Gary is also a Certified Life Coach.

To contact Gary:

- gwlifepursuit@gmail.com

CHAPTER 11

JOY

BY MOHUN SUNDAR

What if someone told you that your success in life had nothing to do with the size of your bank account, intelligence, or physical appearance? What if your true personal and professional success had everything to do with the way you treated yourself and others? How would you define and measure personal and professional success for yourself and others on these terms? In other words, what is your life now worth and why is it worth living?

In an increasingly ambiguous, complex, uncertain, and vulnerable world, it is important that your life's work provide you with a sense of happiness. In today's culture, happiness may be derived from personal and tangible experiences, whether it's the purchase and use of a new product or simply going out on the town to have dinner with friends. Joy represents a more profound sense of happiness where you are able to experience your most positive, intentional, and selfless spiritual energy in the form of shared experiences.

For example, you earn an income mostly due in part to your personal contributions as part of a larger team effort – for those lone wolves out there, I look forward to your letters. Happiness might be derived from the fact that your salary helps to provide material comforts for you and your family. What if your salary was also tied to how many hours of community service you performed or whether your leadership skills were honed by coaching your kids on their homework or attending their sporting events? Would this shift in incentives change your state of mind to decide to renew and redouble your efforts every day at home and at work?

This chapter provides you with a beginning towards a more **joyful** style of living. The techniques and tools listed in this chapter are designed to be practical and straightforward enough to include in your daily lifestyle. Please note that these techniques will take some time to implement and tailor for your lifestyle on a daily and frequent basis. This is about you deciding to permit joy to enter your life and experience a higher level of success in the 21st century economy.

<u>HONESTY</u>

If people are asked if they are honest, most will respond yes to this question in general. However, if they are asked whether they are honest with themselves, they are likely to pause and perhaps provide a less-than-flattering response. Your pathway towards joy begins when you are true to yourself and the values that matter most to you. The fantastic part of this journey is that your sense of joy is already within you. All you need to do is observe your thoughts and separate them from your joyful spirit. At this point, you might be thinking that your experiences and thoughts have led you to here and now, so the mind, body, and soul are one and the same. Most of the time, we're caught up with rationalizing our beliefs, epic wins, hot messes, obligations, and status in life.

The question you need to ask yourself is how much of your daily inner dialogue was actually related to actions that aligned to your sense of joy. Most of the time, you'll find that the dialogue was unproductive and a desperate scramble for total control and self-rationalization of life's unscripted situations. This can lead to outcomes that are detrimental to yourself and others because of a lack of introspection and objectivity. Your most joyful self is wired to do what's best for all in everyday life, so let's activate it now.

Here are some techniques you can use to become more honest with yourself:

The Mirror Routine – Raise your hand or text yourself if you stumble out of bed on most mornings to get ready for the day. You may stumble around preparing and consuming your morning beverage and then begin the day by brushing your teeth, sometimes not in that order—so no judgment on anyone's part. You then proceed with other morning rituals in front of the mirror...this is where TMI (too much information) syndrome can occur. Regardless of your morning rituals in the bathroom, do you ever notice that how your vanity mirror collects a thin layer of dust over time if the mirror is not routinely cleaned. Similarly, your joyful spirit can collect visible and not so visible dust on it if you don't take the time to routinely clean and maintain it. Ultimately, the mirror routine serves as an inroad to creating and understanding your purpose that is highlighted in the next paragraph.

Purpose Exercise – Create purpose in your life by deciding that you're going to be more joyful and start staging a monster comeback by creating meaning (e.g., your family or your hobby) and intentionally taking action on your way to joy. Understand that during this process, there is going to be a level of positive discomfort that exercises your emotional and mental muscles. If your purpose tweet is, "Everything is awesome, I am awesome, mic drop, #joyfulself," then it would be best to rewrite your script and ask yourself what you feel and think about doing with your life, and if you had only a few days or years to live, what would change from your end? A side benefit of rewriting your script is the process of becoming a lifelong learner of yourself and what enables you to create your best and most joyful self. Whatever your method of madness, know that with purpose, you have the ultimate 24/7 energy drink in your hands. Purpose gives you wings.

POSITIVITY

How many people or books have told you that it is important to have a positive mental attitude? And how many of you have told, or wished you could tell, those same people who offered that advice to go to an undesirable location? You're probably inclined to make these types of comments because people don't get you and they don't get your reality. While it is understandable that life's realities, responsibilities, and vagaries can test you on a daily basis, it is important to also find a sense of joy in the present reality. For those of you that always look forward to the endless weekend, it is also important to look forward to this moment and the moment yet to come.

A lot of us stumble out of bed every morning to get things done because deep down you owe it to yourself and others to earn a living, embrace the grind, and enjoy life's small pleasures as time permits. Despite the internal struggle, you may be thinking that there's a lot of good things to notice in a millisecond, but you remember all the minutes and hours that sucked on the way to experience that fleeting moment. Positivity is the state of mind that helps you to shift towards joy by reinforcing your life's purpose every day. Positivity means addressing your reality, believing in yourself and others, and candidly working towards a better and more joyful you.

Here are some techniques you can use to become more honest with yourself:

Gratitude Journal – You may not be able to achieve instant gratification when you read this book, but you can begin the path to instant gratitude when you decide life can work for you and not against you. One of the techniques is to maintain a gratitude journal. Simply put, document the things that make you joyful today and appreciate the awesomeness in your life. There could a second, minute, hour, or entire day of gratitude in your life. Jot down whether there was joyfulness in eating a great meal or your children hugging you for no reason at all.

Self-Talk – This is a complementary technique to the Gratitude Journal. I've found that while the gratitude journal sets a foundation for internal positivity, a little motivational pep talk can reinforce gratitude through the most challenging of days. The key to making this technique work is to find a mantra that works for you and your personality. The great news is that there is so much access to motivational material. If you remain a constant seeker and finder of motivational material, you will ultimately come across something that speaks to you. From there, modify the message to your life's journey.

The Company You Keep – Appreciate having good people around you at all times in your life. Your childhood friends might be a source of support in the initial stages of your life. However, you may need to reexamine these friendships over the course of your life. Are you positively evolving as a human being and are your friends able to evolve at the same rate? Social media is another channel where you can find people who have different personalities but may believe in the same values as you do. However, it is best to know people in person before including them as part of your online social network.

Possibility Thinking – Emphasize 'What If' thinking in your life by going back to your purpose in life and understanding that your goals and outcomes are connected to the story you want to create for yourself. While this may sound like a hokey Hollywood science fiction film, imagine for a second what if your life had no limits and your journey expanded beyond the universe and solar system. I know what you're thinking and you're right – I am only a human being and my goals can only be earthly and realistic. The purpose of this exercise is to get you to think outside the box so that you can dream, inspire, and believe in yourself.

HUMILITY

Part of the feeling of a sense of joy in life is understanding that you are a work-in-progress. I don't mean to say that as a cliché or some way to fill up space in this chapter. It's just part of being human and embracing all of your strengths and imperfections on a daily basis. Every week or month I know that there are conversations that could have been handled better or decisions that should have been better thought out. As a result, I have either someone in my family or in my workplace who might not be positively impacted by it, and the reality sinks in sooner or later. How can you bare your neck and embrace vulnerability and see yourself on the other side of your mountain of courage and humility?

Here are some techniques you can use to improve your level of humility:

24/7/365 Ownership – The first thing to do is to demonstrate total ownership in your life. Own up to your shortcomings, take incremental steps to fix them, and act with courage until you arrive at that moment of truth when you know you've transcended the attitude of blaming others, whining, or defending yourself and start to become more intentional and selfless with your attitude and actions towards others. Keep asking for feedback from people you trust to help get you through those challenging moments. Even if your worst critics keep sending negative feedback your way, treat it as a gift and thank them for the feedback. The best thing you can do is objectively act on the feedback and not be arrogant and self-righteous about the process.

Reflection – This technique ties back to the gratitude journal exercise reviewed earlier in the chapter. How can you better serve and take care of yourself and others without regrets? How would you start your day, week, month, or year in a humbler way? Think about the standards that you would expect from yourself to get to the next level. Ruminate about how you can praise others for their efforts. How can you get back on task with yourself in a way that is forgiving yet demanding? How can you ask your closest family or friends for advice on what they think about handling the everyday decisions and events in life? Ultimately, the purpose of reflection is to allow you the opportunity to develop humility in a non-judgmental and transparent way.

About Mohun Sundar

Mohun Sundar intends to help people discover their inner sense of happiness and purpose in life. Born and raised in Northern California during the advent of the online economy, Mohun is now looking to launch a career as an author and speaker on how people can discover their most authentic and joyful version of themselves in a dynamic global economy.

Mohun attained a bachelor's degree from UC Santa Barbara and a graduate degree from Penn State University. He currently serves as a project manager and has more than ten years of education and experience in the health care industry. In addition, he has earned multiple project management accreditations. He is looking to apply the interpersonal, knowledge, and trust building skills acquired in the workplace into his initial foray as an entrepreneur.

When he isn't pursuing his professional goals, Mohun enjoys playing and watching basketball and tennis in his spare time. He is also an active member of his local Toastmasters chapter and enjoys talking to others about how they can improve their public speaking skills. In addition, Mohun has a keen interest for discussing and learning about the latest global leadership and innovation trends.

You can connect with Mohun at:

- https://www.linkedin.com/in/mohunsundar
- https://twitter.com/mohunsundar1

CHAPTER 12

FROM ENGINEER TO EMPIRE

BY TIM REID

When I was a little boy, my Mom was a single parent doing the very best she could. She told me to do well in school, get into a good college, get a good career, and that is how you became successful. Being the only member of my mother's side of the family to ever go on to post-secondary education (we were a farming family from small town Ontario), I did my best to follow her advice, and by most standards of society would be considered "successful" as a telecommunications engineer. I had the big corporate job with the security, benefits, and paid vacation that many strive for. That said, I had to book my entire year's vacation in January every year, get called out at 2:00 am to customer sites, and my income never kept pace with my skills. Was this all there was to corporate life in Canada?

I was not getting to where I wanted to go as fast as I wanted to get there, and decided that having someone else dictate my schedule was not for me. I did not realize it at the time, but I had discovered one of the first keys to success: *making decisions and sticking to them.* It was at that moment I decided to become a student of wealth creation. I read any book I could get my hands on about how to become highly successful and achieve financial freedom, while at the time not even having a firm grasp of this concept. After extensive research on the topic, I learned there are three methods ultra-successful people have used to create financial freedom: stocks, businesses, and real estate. Real Estate was the method that appealed to me most because I had always been intrigued by how Donald Trump had achieved his level of success in business.

Regardless of your political beliefs, reading a few of Trumps books led me to a seminar about how to make money in real estate. After leaving that seminar, I knew that real estate was the business for me in which to create financial freedom. I did not however, know how to become an entrepreneur, or where the 7-year roller coaster ride I was about to embark on would take me. It was through this journey into the jungle of real estate investing and down the rocky road of business ownership that I would find my true "why," and the destination I was headed for, which had become lost along the way up the corporate ladder.

There are only so many rungs you can climb on that corporate ladder in a certain period of time. This slow ascent was what drove me into all of that research in the first place, leading me to create my first real estate corporation, doing over one million dollars of real estate transactions each year since its inception in 2010. I stayed committed to that learning, attending many seminars, workshops, masterminds, courses, and trainings of all kinds to enhance the skills I already had, and to learn new ones to keep my business moving forward. This was the second success secret I learned: *a commitment to constant learning is key.* I had experienced this in my field of telecom, where I was constantly sent on courses to keep up on the new technologies I needed to be implementing for clients. This fact holds true in the business world as well. I am proud and a little bit shocked to report that I have invested over $100,000 in my business and real estate education over the last seven years – money well spent down to the last dime! I could not imagine where I would be without all of the knowledge, experience, and connections that those opportunities have given me over the years.

Through these educational experiences I discovered the world of personal growth, and I had no idea the link that existed between the "inner game" and the "outer game" – put simply, the relationship between what goes on between your ears and your results in the physical world! The thoughts and feelings that you have in your mind, are a direct reflection of your success and results in your life. Further, the only person responsible for the place you are at, is the person staring back at you in the mirror, yes that's right – you!

Once you take accountability for your circumstances you have the power to change your outcomes. Complaining and whining about it will only keep you where you are, and not creating the positive change you truly want. I had been stuck in my own head about a few things, such as the economy being bad, so that was why I had not received the promotion or the wage increases I wanted – which was utter BS. To be clear, I could have changed my outcomes years earlier had I known about this concept - that you could create your OWN economy by becoming a business owner.

This point is worth expanding on because the corporate job is supposed to be the one with "security," but as we see with more and more examples such as the death of NORTEL, working for a large company is never truly secure because something unexpected could happen, and people could get let go or the company could go under. Some people also climb that corporate ladder for many years only to realize the ladder is standing against the wrong tower of success – the things at the top aren't the things they truly want! This leads me to the concept of your "why" – why do you want to become successful? What if you had all the money you could ever need, what would you do then?

That question was something I had never asked myself until going through all of those seminars and events. The conclusion

I came to was that I wanted to help others avoid the scarcity I felt growing up in a single parent home. I had everything I needed – let's be clear – my mother did a great job providing and teaching me the core values required to become the person I am, and I am thankful for the journey I have had so far, otherwise I would not be the same person I am today. My mission is to help further the financial education of as many people as I can around the world, because I believe that is where a lot of the problems that our society faces began; people not having the resources they need to take care of themselves and their families.

Through our training, coaching, and consulting, I am on a mission to change the financial futures of as many families as possible, and I would not be able to work on that mission full time unless I was open to opportunity. This was the third secret to success I learned: *You have to always maintain an open mind to the opportunities that are all around you.* I left the corporate world, in arguably one of the worst real estate markets in Alberta's history, to run my business full time – many would call that crazy, I saw an opportunity. I realized that the time I was spending on the corporate life was strangling the progress for the business, and after making that shift I went from one company with two divisions to five companies with thirteen divisions – spanning three different industries! Maintaining a mindset of success, opportunities started to appear around every corner and the right people started showing up in my life to make those opportunities possible.

Having very specific goals was also critical to my accelerated success. One exercise I recommend is to have a vision board. Write down ten goals that you are really passionate about achieving; the dream car you always wanted, the trip of a lifetime, the house you have always wanted – then cut out pictures or print them off from the internet and stick them up on a board in a place where you can see it every morning and every night before you go to sleep. This constant reminder of what your destination looks like when you have accomplished your major success goals will do two things: first, it will help keep you motivated when you get knocked off course, and second, it will help program your subconscious mind to work on solutions to the challenges you will face along your journey to accomplishing them. This simple exercise will change your life, and it can be found it many books on success and wealth creation. Why? Because it works! A trainer I once saw stated it this way: "Please don't try to make the wheel any rounder!" Just follow the system! I have also found that writing down ten goals each morning before I start my day gets me fired up to get to work on taking the steps that I know will get me closer to achieving them.

One of the lessons I have learned travelling down the road of a business owner is that you have to make the decision that you are going to do things differently than you ever have before and take risks. Taking risks is a scary thing to do – and that is natural. Our instincts are programmed to keep us safe (in the same place without changing) which happens to be just on this side of having everything you have ever wanted after obtaining financial freedom. There will always be challenges, whether you take the leap of faith and make a significant change or not. Why not take the chance, believe in yourself, and that you deserve more and go for it? Ask yourself what is the worst that could happen? Could you not go back to the way things were? I have never heard a story of a man or a woman being on their death bed – when asked about what they regret – stating they were worried about the things they DID - they were a lot more concerned about the things they DID NOT DO!

I had a great time in the corporate world for over a decade, however, I realized along the way that I had settled and made up excuses for why things were not going to change. Through a personal breakup, I realized settling does not result in happiness in any area of your life – you have to always be growing, learning, and challenging yourself to be truly excited and fulfilled in life. That concept worked in tandem with the fact that I wound up doing work I was no longer having fun with. "The day that the fun died" was the 90-day countdown to my committing to making a career change. You see, I was interested in making a change for a long time before that, however I was not COMMITTED to taking the actions necessary until what I was doing was no longer fun. I encourage you to learn from my experience here and take action before the pain of staying the same outweighs the pain or fear of making the changes needed to get you moving toward your goals.

I think we all know the importance of setting goals. There are entire books written about this topic – but what do the goals support? Having goals is critical to success, but what lies at the end of them being accomplished? What are you truly passionate about? A cause, making an impact, leaving a legacy, being recognized? It is equally important to have something you are truly passionate about to keep the fire blazing inside of you, to keep you up at night to near obsession so that you are always growing. Having all of those lists of goals checked off, and then having nothing to keep you excited is all too common in our society.

I have personally met some ultra-wealthy, very successful people who are negative, miserable, and without direction. The ingredient missing from those individuals' lives is that burning desire to keep doing something they are truly passionate about – what is that thing for you? I encourage you to get out a sheet of paper and write that one thing down, even if you already know what it is – it could change over time and that's ok. Putting pen to paper has a powerful way of cementing that concept into your subconscious. Brian's advice to "think on paper" has helped me a great deal over the years, and I know it will help you on your journey as well.

Everything that has ever existed in our world started out as a thought in someone else's mind. Take a moment and ponder that fact. This concept is proof that anything you can imagine can be made real in the physical reality if you commit to it 100% for an extended period if time. Henry Ford said it best: "whether you think you can, or you think you can't, you're right". Having the mindset of successful people is one of the most impactful skills I have cultivated and has been the game changer along my pathway to success. Like tending to a seedling that will turn into a mighty oak tree one day – a millionaire mindset needs to be tended to every day. Through meditation, reading, and watching only motivational, educational, and positive materials, you will reinforce a healthy and supportive mind.

Success starts within the six inches between your ears. You need to protect that space from negative news, negative people, and negative influences surrounding circumstances that you can't control. There is a concept I like to call "mental bandwidth" (you can take the engineer out of the lab but can't take the lab out of the engineer!), which means the available energy you have to spend on the challenges of each day. This bandwidth is finite – so you have to choose wisely what you spend it on each day. If you spend that precious bandwidth on things you can't control (negativity, unsupportive activities/people) then you will not have any left to spend on success and supportive activity that gets you closer to your goals!

I am a farm kid from small town Ontario, and I have had a heck of a ride from the ivory tower to the freedom of an Entrepreneur. I am excited every day when I get up knowing that I get to help others achieve higher levels of success. If I can take that leap off of the corporate tower and survive, you can too – if you're thinking about making that jump, you are on the right track. Never settle!

I look forward to hearing your story one day.
Respect The Hustle,
Tim Reid, The Lifestyle Engineer

About Tim

Tim Reid is a Sophisticated Real Estate Investor, Real Estate Investing Mentor, Author, Speaker, Entrepreneur, and Telecommunications Engineer turned "Lifestyle Engineer." He is the creator of the #1 Real Estate Business Success System, a 7-step system to one million dollars in real estate transactions in 12 months or less.

Born in the Ottawa Valley area of southern Ontario, Tim worked his way up the corporate ladder with a multi-national corporation of over 4,000 employees, operating in over 150 countries for over a decade. During this time, Tim founded Phoenix Real Estate Investing Inc., finding his passion for real estate investing.

In 2015, he added a training/coaching division to the Phoenix Real Estate group after seeing a huge lack of top-notch real estate training options for Canadians. Built on the principles of integrity, community, networking, and working together, Tim has expanded the Phoenix Real Estate group to operate and conduct business in over ten markets in North America.

Then in February of 2016, Tim decided to leave the corporate world to run the Phoenix Group full time, which has expanded into other businesses such as commercial development, a restaurant, private investment fund management, a car dealership, and most recently Phoenix Marketing; a full-service agency providing guidance on Branding/Marketing to Entrepreneurs.

Tim's no-nonsense approach, transparency in business, and expertise in real estate, has attracted clients from all walks of life to join his programs, delivering results in real estate and giving Canadians the tools they need to secure their financial futures for their families.

A published author and regular contributor to real estate magazines, Tim was recently interviewed by CBC News and Global TV. He is an expert columnist for *Business Edge Magazine*, and is currently involved with two books. Within his first two years of running the Phoenix Real Estate group, Tim was named Investor of the Year by a National Real Estate club.

Tim has executed real estate deals netting over $250,000 in profit and has transacted over seven million dollars of real estate in seven short years. Specializing in the creative side of real estate, he is extremely passionate about helping others learn the skills they need to build wealth in this arena, avoiding the pitfalls many new *and* experienced investors face. Canada's leading expert in Relationship Marketing, he teaches the system behind helping monetize and exponentially grow your business income, and network in any vertical.

Tim currently lives in Calgary, Alberta, Canada with his amazing girlfriend of six years. He makes helping his fellow Canadians find their pathway to financial freedom his #1 priority.

To contact Tim Reid:

- 1-403-246-4409
- 1-587-225-2643
- treid@phoenixrealestateinvesting.com
- www.phoenixrealestateinvesting.com

CHAPTER 13

DON'T LET THE BIG P GET YOU!

BY WYATT KLINGERMAN

Twenty years from now you will be more disappointed by the things that you didn't do than by the ones you did do ... Sail away from the safe harbor. Catch the trade winds in your sails. Explore. Dream. Discover.
~ Mark Twain

In college, I took a Music 101 class. In this most unlikely of unlikely classes, I learned an unexpected life lesson. As I sat in the music room on that Fall semester morning, I could have never predicted I would receive a piece of wisdom I would never forget. I share this wisdom with whoever will hold still long enough to listen.

In walked the professor, an elderly man we'd come to know simply as "Doc." Doc was a man of small stature, but huge presence. He strode confidently into the room, took his position at the front of the class, where he used a music stand as a lectern. From there, he looked about the room, peering over the top of his glasses, as he locked eyes with each student, one by one. He took roll, as is customary on the first day, but when he concluded with the ordinary is when he began the extraordinary.

He turned his back to the class, snatched up a piece of chalk, and with great artistic flair, he wrote the letter "P" on the chalkboard. This was not written as you or I would write it. The chalkboard could barely contain the symbolism and enormity of this giant letter. After taking a moment to admire his handiwork, he spun to face the class, vigorously tapped the chalkboard with the chalk, and warned, "Don't let the Big P get you!"

The class responded with stunned, awkward silence, followed by a few juvenile giggles from the back. He stood steadfast and stared out at us over his glasses. I thought to myself, "Was this music theory?" Having spent years playing a variety of musical instruments, I couldn't seem to connect the dots. This wasn't familiar, at all. What was I missing? I sat forward in my chair, intrigued. His gaze combed through the room and finally came around to me, and he locked on. I must have looked like I ate that expired egg salad sandwich from the hallway vending machine.

He rapped the chalkboard, again, and repeated his warning. "Don't let the Big P get you. It will ruin your life." This new warning was even more dire! The classroom was so quiet, one couldn't help but focus on Doc, or wonder if everyone else had escaped. He pointed at me, and my confused mug, and asked, "What is the Big P?" Oh, how I wouldn't wish that uncomfortable level of pressure on anyone! My mind raced through every P-word I knew. Ultimately, fear of being wrong pushed me to answer with the almighty shield of ignorance… "Eh, I don't know."

"Procrastination. Procrastination will ruin your life. Don't let the Big P get you."

That lesson has followed me, from that day on. But it didn't end there. He was a living public service message. He had wisdom to share, and he didn't hesitate to do so. Procrastination is a devastating force, robbing people from fulfilling their potential in life.

So, what driving force can we implement to beat back the Big P? Beyond the obvious and useless, "don't procrastinate," which is right up there with "Don't set yourself on fire," "Don't put that plastic bag over your head," and "Don't eat that egg salad sandwich from the hallway vending machine," we must take action. Better yet, we must take Decisive Action. Gads! Decision-making!

If you listen carefully, you can hear a chorus of moans. Why is this? Well, people loathe making decisions, because decision points are forks in life's road. To make a decision is to select one direction in that fork, to the exclusion of all others. This can be a tough habit to form, especially for those who like to "keep their options open." This is like being in a boat on a still lake, but refusing to put our oars in the water. Like anything in life, we must create good habits to replace the bad habits.

How do we start down this exciting new path? Great question! It just so happens, our old buddy, Doc, had some sage wisdom in that regard. In one of my discussions with him, Doc shared this advice. "Be swift and decisive in all decisions of little consequence. Be more deliberate in your decision making in those of more consequence. But always make those decisions and keep moving forward." Marinate in that for a moment. How many times have we pushed someone else to make a simple, inconsequential decision we didn't want to make? What do you feel like doing? What movie do you want to watch? Where do you want to go to eat? None of these decisions will matter, come tomorrow, so why is putting the decision in another's hands so common?

Letting others decide is the easiest solution for decision-dodgers. This may give that sense of ease they seek, but in their eyes, this tactic also eliminates their responsibility in the matter. If things don't turn out the way they wish, they can blame the responsible decision-making party. This is a weak position, setting up a lifetime of disheartening disappointment. Being the

129

captains of our own ships, as we chart life's waters, gives us the greatest chance of arriving at our chosen destinations. Allowing others to steer our ships, hoping they will guide us to our desired ports, makes us captives. The reality for this tactic is more in line with being a stowaway on someone else's ship. This creates directionless hopelessness, which leads into a downward spiral of negativity. Be a captain, not a captive.

The key to these inconsequential decisions is to make them, walk down that fork, and move on with our lives. It's easy to play guide in the jungle of inconsequential decisions. Just pick that movie, restaurant, or activity. Grab your safari hat and lead the way. Doing so sets you on the path to making better decisions in all areas of life.

On the flip side of that coin are the major forks in life's road. This is where we should take the time to check our compasses before proceeding down a selected path. However, in keeping with the need to take decisive action, we must select a path at the fork. Life doesn't pause while we pitch a tent and set camp at the fork. Life will pass us by. The decisions we didn't make, and the actions we didn't take, will transform into the regrets we take with us for the rest of our lives.

But, wait! That's a great piece of inspirational wisdom (albeit a bit wordy for a bumper sticker), but what if the selected fork leads to failure? This is a valid concern shared by hundreds of millions if not billions of people and is the main cause of paralysis by analysis, or what I like to call perpetual preparation. The goals we seek will be on our to-do lists, forever. Although we may be well-intentioned and appear quite busy in preparing to take the desired fork in the road, we can't bring ourselves to start walking.

In short, avoid perpetual preparation! This is like a train that never leaves the station for its destination! Alright, what if we pick a path, start to walk, and that path leads to failure? *I will let you in on a secret: failure doesn't exist.* Trial and error, learning and growing, and improving through perseverance is all that really exists. In fact, we learn more and grow more from any errors we make. No one has ever sprinted forth from the womb with the agility of a cat, not even cats!

The concept of failure is learned, and must be unlearned. For example, you fell down countless times, as you learned to stand and walk and run. The thought of failure never occurred to you while you were trying to become bipedal. At no point did anyone tell you to "Give up," or "You're not good enough," or that "You're destined to be a quadruped like the family dog." You were only learning how to succeed through trial and error. Taking decisive action, and continuing to march forward, brings you back to this path toward success.

Decisive action obliterates the Big P and plunges the action-taker into the most valuable of learning environments. Some say one only "fails" when one gives up, but I would argue, not even then, since the lessons learned are valuable. Once a mistake is made, and the lesson learned, one is unlikely to make that same mistake, again. Dedication toward success leads to success. Walk in faith and take the plunge, knowing you will continue to learn and grow and adapt and reach your goals.

Taking decisive action creates its own momentum. Forward momentum instills purpose and inflames passion and drive. Often, it's those first few steps that are the most challenging. Once we gain momentum, the obstacles encountered will be viewed in a new way. What steps can be taken to bypass the obstacle? What is the solution to a particular problem? Over, around, under, or through, we must bypass obstacles and always move forward. There is always a way. Find it. Never stop. Never be stopped. To achieve success is to not settle for less. No fighter ever stepped into the ring and whined about not winning because the opponent fought back. Champions make decisions, formulate plans, and implement strategies. And when knocked down, they get back up.

Whether we're looking to take our businesses to the next level or still dreaming about starting one, we're faced with the same leap into the deep end of the pool. We can plan and analyze and prepare, but we have to jump in at some point to move toward our goals. We have to get in the pool if we want to swim. Getting dressed for the occasion just won't cut it. We'll have to adjust to the water temperature and depth, once we're in up to our necks. Planning and preparation are essential, but the dirty little secret is that anything we do in life is like prepping for war. It is all set and meticulously planned until the first shot is fired. Then, everything changes as new plans are formulated and adjustments are made on the fly.

Our lives, and what we choose to do with them, are limited only by the restrictions we place upon ourselves. Even avoidance of a decision is ultimately a decision to do nothing. When someone expresses an unsatisfactory situation in life, I tend to try to help and make suggestions. However, when my assistance is met with a list of never-ending excuses, I reverse course and offer a sympathetic ear. Excuses strike me as scapegoats for a perfectly capable person to justify self-imposed limitations. I call this: Riding in the Excuse Caboose. It's always a bumpy ride that guarantees to be the last to arrive at the destination, if at all. Be the engineer in the Engine, not the white-knuckled whiner in the Excuse Caboose!

As the Pareto Principle has taught us: in life, preparation amounts to 20% and decisive action accounts for 80%. Learning what we need to accomplish certain goals is only part of the equation. Taking decisive action to implement that knowledge is the key. That is where we focus our energies to make measurable progress toward our goals and, ultimately, our dreams. No one wants to give up on their dreams. After all, our dreams are among the few things in life worth waking up for. So make those decisions and, more importantly, take those actions. And for God's sake, don't let the Big P get you!

About Wyatt

With a keen eye on the future, an unquenchable thirst for knowledge, and an imaginative mind (filled with crazy ideas) Wyatt Klingerman often jokes about being roughly four and a half minutes ahead of his time.

Born with an overactive imagination, Wyatt naturally gravitated towards creative pursuits. After studying filmmaking and directing, he fell in love with writing and the creative chaos of storytelling.

When he's not staring off into space, lost in a tale he's writing, or carrying on lengthy conversations with his horses, Wyatt can be found playing the guitar, wandering museums, or researching information on the latest topic of interest. A ridiculously positive and supportive person, Wyatt is a firm believer that the impossible just takes a little longer.

After decades of study in the art of storytelling, Wyatt founded Professional Daydreamers. He coaches and teaches writers of all levels his macro approach to storytelling. He believes in teaching writers "How to write, not what to write." With a fun and immersive teaching style, he helps writers amass and become proficient in an arsenal of writing techniques.

Wyatt feels all writers can pursue their passions and successfully write the stories of their dreams, once armed with a working knowledge to implement a vast array of story tools. Common story problems and related difficulties make this most challenging of fine arts even more so, but these obstacles to success can be obliterated with the right knowledge.

With loyal support, Wyatt guides his clients toward professional-level writing. His students take a fun and informative journey that bypasses the usual information overwhelm and gets writers the usable skills they seek in a swift and effective manner.

You can connect with Wyatt at:

- www.ProfessionalDaydreamers.com

CHAPTER 14

FINALLY HAPPY *AND* RICH!

BY BIANCA DAUBER

How do you move beyond feeling like you never have enough? We seem to be surrounded by scarcity, as far as the eye can see. Bills demand to be paid, you only pay yourself half the salary you promised yourself, while your employees are heading off on vacation for the second time this year. It's enough to make us cry. Not that we'd tell them they couldn't take their well-earned vacation. Quite the contrary. But this, once again, shows us the ugly face of the lack of funds, because we can no longer remember what it means to take a vacation.

But WE'RE supposed to be the entrepreneurs! After all, we create jobs, pay wages, and make sure that the store is up and running every day. But all too often we don't even get to collect whatever pitiful profits there might be, given the taxes and other bills that never seem to go away. Why is this the case?! Something has gone tremendously wrong! We bear the risk, spend 24/7 worrying about the company, only to once again sincerely wish our employees a nice vacation, while secretly crying on the inside out of envy. That is BS! And yet we are stuck in the middle of it, every day the same nonsense. Yesterday we thought it couldn't get any worse, but today we were proven wrong.

We have to put a stop to this once and for all! Finally!

We're doing a good job, thinking of ways to improve our business every day and better position ourselves on the market. And, last but not least, our private life suffers immensely, while others enjoy a delicious dinner by the sea. Not jealousy, but a terribly ugly mirror, which is maliciously held up to our noses by life.

We came to this world to be here for a while, as meaningfully as possible, as happy and healthy as possible. But if we only experience deficiency and drag ourselves from one obstacle to the next, we are doing something quite wrong. We're not going with the flow, but choosing the torrential counterflow, which throws us back again and again. And we fight and fight for every inch of it, only to painfully realize that we are slogging along in the wrong direction. The river naturally flows from the small spring into the big, wide sea - a company preferably from the first idea (source) to the big success (sea). Preferably. It could be so nice. If only we didn't spend all our time putting the cart before the horse. Why do we make it so difficult for ourselves? Because we try hopping on one leg instead of walking on both!

The universe rewards those who go with the flow. There is a power that leads us all unerringly if only we allow it and don't fight it. We just have to allow ourselves to acknowledge this truth. Most of us believe in some form of higher intellect, higher power, or deity. However you say it, most of us know that there is something there that is greater and more powerful than we are. And on the other hand, we live in a world governed by material things and rules that lure us into a web of dependency and at the same time we often struggle with it.

We find ourselves longing for a deep attachment to this higher power, while finding ourselves seemingly helpless in the face of all these material obligations and needs. We crave fulfillment and don't realize that the next purchase is only going to pull us further and further into the maelstrom of attachment. But then, after some reflection, we come to see the material world as just some crazy hamster wheel from which we have to escape. We meditate regularly, immerse ourselves in some deep books, and begin to believe that we now embody that wisdom. At least for a while. Until the unpaid bills pile up and we forget about that.

We are trying, we want to do everything right. But what is right? No idea, we think, and simply carry on. You can't have anything without money. So we plunge back into the fray, the career coming first. Meditating is overrated anyway. The finances are beginning to look good again, but still we're not really satisfied. No matter. We pay our bills on time, eat chic food and spend money until the doctor comes. So it goes. But something's missing. And again the hamster wheel rolls on.

Over the years I have come across two types of people again and again. The first are workaholic entrepreneurs, outwardly successful and wealthy, but apparently dissatisfied. In addition, their companies often had to struggle financially. The second are spiritual freelancers who carried the precious seeds for a more meaningful version of themselves, striving to develop them. However, they invariably had problems with their finances. Even if they could ignore it for a while under the guise of personal development, they eventually got caught up with the brutal reality of being in the red.

I know from countless examples how difficult and incompatible it seems to live a spiritual AND a prosperous life. For a long time, I myself was one of you – between both sides, sometimes on one, then on the other – for many years unable to find a balance, much less to live it. Are spiritual people better than those chasing after material possessions? Our egos spin an arrogant web of hidden vanity and misunderstood wisdom.

Or are entrepreneurs the be-all and end-all? Is not prosperity and the pursuit of it the only truth to which all our ambitions should apply? Actually, almost everything in life is about money. Therefore, it cannot hurt to accumulate a good amount of it.

We are not here to lose touch with reality in hours of meditation. Also, we are not better people when we live in poverty and starve ourselves for the sake of calling ourselves spiritual. And neither are we here to chase after the filthy lucre on a straight path to hell. The main thing is that our money bags are full, this is understood.

It is not fulfilling to go one way or the other. Then we negate a piece of us that is an integral part of our humanity. Through this separation, we cause our first financial problems. We have to manage ourselves, our longing for a bond with a higher intelligence and our balance of accounts.

What appears to be polarity is really a cry for unification! *How do we achieve this?*

If you want to live in a modern industrialized society and not like a yogi in the Himalayas, then the best way for a holistic life is to unite spirituality and prosperity!

Spirituality is the path of self-inquiry and self-knowledge and has nothing to do with esotericism. . . and prosperity and wealth are, of course, not limited to financial concerns.

You want to be a better person, but you also have to live off of something. And you should live WELL! It is crucial to integrate spirituality by anchoring it in the material aspects of daily life. I can promise you, it is WONDERFUL to have a life that is both spiritually and materially successful! Yes, from today onward you can be both spiritual AND rich! You can connect to the source and draw from it.

So let us allow it and learn to listen to the simple language of the universe. We can take up a new life that will shower us with riches. And once we have tasted the fruits that suddenly fall so easily into our laps, we will wonder why we've spent so much time fighting, doubting, and waiting.

What does this mean in practice?

Of course, having a fulfilling life or a successful business means more than being in touch with a higher power and having a healthy checkbook. That's very clear. Unfortunately, this chapter is not the place for holistic implementation plans, but here are a few first steps that you can easily integrate into your everyday life:

<u>Spirituality</u>

1. Open yourself to the idea that there is something perceptible outside of us that is infinitely greater than us and guides us.

2. Turn off your phone and get ready to enjoy TV-free evenings.

3. Take leaps and bounds with Ayurvedic nutritional supplements, for example.

4. Pay attention to your dreams: they have meaning and can be valuable guides.

5. Dare to read a spiritual book.

6. Appreciate yourself and others.

7. Enjoy yoga, take a walk in nature, give yourself time for rest and contemplation.

8. Start meditating; five minutes in the morning or evening is a great start.

9. Pay close attention to your breath, practice pranayama (breathing exercises).

10. Turn off electrical equipment you're not using. It is all the easier to tune in to the original, natural energy the less we are surrounded by artificial radiation. Time spent in nature is where we recharge our true batteries.

Open yourself to the idea of the connections between the inside and the outside. Keep your eyes and ears open and listen to the silent clues for the right direction. You will be guided. A higher intelligence guides us all. Open yourself bit by bit, let it happen. The "proof of this theory" that your mind so craves will come to you through external experiences that lead you quietly. And "I think it is possible" will, over time, become an inner knowledge that allows no more doubts.

But beware, because it is not just the right vibration that achieves this. It's not enough to make yourself comfortable in front of the TV, and no one's managed to build a house yet through constant meditation. That's simply not how it works. What use is all this cosmic guidance if we do not make active use of the energy? We need to get up and do something. Otherwise, things would quickly get boring.

And so, we come to the second pillar of a good life: your finances. (Ha, if somebody told me years ago that I'd develop such a soft spot on the subject, I would have been rolling on the floor laughing.) …☺

Prosperity

1. Open yourself to the idea that your external financial situation is linked to your inner convictions. There is no separation.

2. Open yourself to the idea that you create your own financial situation. You are not a victim and not helpless, at the mercy of circumstances. Whether consciously or unconsciously, YOU create it.

3. Do not judge yourself or others for certain deficiencies, they just want to steer you in a better direction.

4. Recognize those external obstacles that recur as valuable hints on inner blockages – lacking convictions or a wrong

direction.

5. Check your thoughts about money and wealthy people. Are you benevolent or envious? Allow others to be happy; you'll then find it easier for yourself to be happy.

6. Tally up your books. Face the facts and take a hard look at your finances.

7. Be aware of where you want to go financially.

8. Live a win-win-win life; be fair to yourself, your employees, and your customers.

9. Give back - this is probably the best side effect of prosperity. If you have a lot, you can give a lot. And the more you give, the more you will get so that you can keep on giving.

10. You need a simple and clearly-structured financial management system. Nothing works without it! At least not permanently. Financial management is fun! Just follow a clear and efficient financial management system and put your life and your business on a sound footing from now on. Stick to it for the long haul, starting immediately on day one! This is the most important part when it comes to taking action, finally doing something solid.

THE WANT OF YESTERDAY WILL BE THE ABUNDANCE OF TOMORROW!

It's not important that you believe in it. The important thing is that you think it is POSSIBLE.

Pay attention to BOTH sides of a good life! Start at a point that is easy for you. The change already begins with the first step. It's a lot easier than you might think. Then take the next one and you'll see it's worth it. The more you can incorporate it into your everyday life, the faster you will see success. It will take off like a rocket. With each step, your life will experience more transformation towards a richer life. Inside and out.

Another important tip:

Embrace and live gratitude. Gratitude is an incredibly underrated concept. It is the guarantor for more flow in your life. Take the small changes that happen as proof. Be grateful and, I promise you, it will seem like magic! Because what you can be grateful for will increase, like magic. Your life will definitely be better and more fulfilled. That's a promise.

So get started and lure wealth and all its magical facets into your life.

GET HIGH ON THE CREATIVE POWER!
GET HIGH ON YOURSELF!

About Bianca

Bianca's goal is to help entrepreneurs and individuals lead fulfilling and prosperous lives. For more than 20 years, she has devoted herself intensively to the study of finance and the integration of spirituality into everyday life. Her mission is to inspire and help people to live in their higher self – based in purpose, beauty and abundance.

Bianca is a trained TV presenter and worked for several years in front of the camera at Grundy Light Entertainment for Kabel 1, ProSiebenSat.1 Media AG she has appeared on. As a model, she traveled the world very successfully for several years. She got to know and appreciate diverse cultures in different countries; however, she did not feel comfortable in this often superficial world of modeling.

Born in the former East Germany, she loved writing and exploring meaningful questions and the causes of inner and outer perceptions and experiences. She felt a great yearning for self-realization and began intensive self-exploration early on; later, she also practiced in India and with Yogi Cameron from the USA. Today, she lives with the spiritual sadhana (practice) integrated into her normal everyday life as a businesswoman.

After attaining a high-school diploma and business management qualification following a chief executive, Bianca decided, while pursuing her business and economics studies, to leap into entrepreneurship. At the age of 23, Bianca founded her first company. She developed various concepts for media formats, including a nationwide modeling contest for a large German company and implemented it in cooperation with media partners and an international modeling agency.

Three years later, Bianca founded her second company in the wellness industry with ten employees. As the sole owner of her company, she went through the school of hard knocks financially. High investment costs, a drastic economic downturn as a result of the introduction of the euro, and a lack of experience at her young age led to a threatening financial situation for her company. But giving up was not an option. Driven by this corporate crisis, she expanded her studies in finance and the influence of our subconscious on it. She designed an effective financial management system and refined it over the years through hands-on application. Not only did she save her company from bankruptcy, she also led it to become one of the most successful in the industry for eleven years.

Since 2012, Bianca and her partner have been very successfully developing and selling their own product lines with growing revenues in the seven-digit range. Bianca has gone from $750,000 in debt to a thriving million-dollar business.

Several serious personal losses, which left their marks on her, have also made her a strong and successful woman. For more than 15 years, Bianca has been involved in various charitable organizations.

At the time of this writing, she is setting up her own foundation, the Andy & Bianca Dauber Foundation 'Sibling Hearts', to commemorate her beloved brother Andy, and thus fulfill her heart's desire.

You can connect and visit the author online at:

- contact@biancadauber.com
- www.BiancaDauber.com
- www.Immobilien-Investorin.de
- www.Stiftung-Geschwisterherzen.de (foundation)

Bianca stands for the unification of spirituality and abundance, and her deep conviction is:

'Who wants to achieve highs, should be able to go in depths.'

CHAPTER 15

CRACKING THE CODE TO EMAIL MARKETING

BY LINDSAY DICKS

Ever since the first email program was developed way back in 1971, email has become one of our chief communication tools. With over 205 billion emails sent and received each day, it's still an essential tool for marketers to share information with current and prospective customers.

It wasn't always easy, though. Kids today will never experience the excitement and anticipation of listening to the hiss and whine of a telephone modem connecting to the Internet. They'll never understand the joy of paying for Internet access by the minute instead of by gigabytes, or the frustration of spending your minutes downloading an inbox full of spam. Just think how bored they would be if they couldn't send pictures with their emails. Such was the Internet during those heady days of the 1990s.

EMAIL IS STILL RELEVANT

Fast forward to today and email is still with us and going strong. Some media experts believe email will be replaced as early as 2020 by some yet-to-be-named website or app. Don't believe it. Oh sure, 100 years from now, marketers may look back at email like we view the horse and buggy today – quaint, yet crude. But the numbers just can't be ignored. Email use is still on the rise, averaging an increase of 3 percent each year.

Sure, social media has changed the dynamic for how we interact electronically with consumers. Of course, using email and social media is not an either/or proposition. The best e-marketing plans include email, Twitter, Facebook, and any number of other social media sites. But keep in mind, email has been shown to convert more contacts to customers by an almost 2-to-1 margin.

Email marketers today also need to be aware of the mobile revolution. Almost half of all emails are opened on a mobile device. Just like your website needs to be responsive to multiple devices, your emails should be adaptable to tablets and smartphones. Some steps you can take to ensure readability include:

- Increasing font size so the copy is easier to read on a small screen

- Making the call-to-action buttons larger for easy tapping

- Designing the email in a single column for easy scrolling

COMPETING WITH SPAM AND SCAMS

Two of the biggest obstacles for marketers to overcome are having their emails considered spam, the electronic version of junk mail, or email scams trying to defraud recipients or infect their computers.

All email marketers must comply with the CAN-SPAM Act passed in 2003. A few of the more relevant aspects of the law for legitimate marketing purposes stipulate that the emails:

- **Include an unsubscribe link**

- **Feature subject lines that relate directly to the content in the email**

- **Contain content with at least one sentence, not just a link**

If you want to get fancy, the technical term for spam is Unsolicited Commercial Email, or UCE. Some studies estimate anywhere from 65-78 percent of emails sent each day are spam. How do you make sure your email stands out from all the clutter? To better understand that, we first need to understand how a spam filter works and how to avoid ending up in the dreaded spam folder.

There are numerous spam filters available today. Simple ones search the subject heading and email content for suspicious words, such as "Viagra," and check to see if they contain words in ALL CAPS, misspellings, and multiple exclamation points!!! Some look at the IP address of the originating email. If the email service has received spam from the IP address previously, other legitimate emails coming from that IP address could also be labeled as spam. Others check out complex sounding things like Reverse DNS Lookup, Domain Keys and IP Throttling to make sure the emails are legit.

There's no way to guarantee your marketing emails will never be flagged as spam, but there are steps you can follow to help your emails reach the inbox:

- **Communicate at regular intervals** – Don't wait six months between emails. Your recipients will be less likely to remember you. First, you have to decide what constitutes a regular interval for your emails. Above all, keep it relevant. It's easy for a retailer to send out emails about sales or new products, but what can an accountant do besides sending a reminder about April 15? Think about what's on your calendar that your followers might be interested in. The accountant could keep people updated on the late filing deadline, a reminder to submit flexible spending account receipts, and any changes to IRS regulations.

- **Segment your list** – Depending on your business, you may want to divide your email list into different interest groups. A pet store would want to segment the pet owners on their list by animal. A cat owner that receives offers geared toward dog owners may get fed up and unsubscribe or report your emails as spam.

- **Use a third-party provider** – Companies dedicated to processing marketing emails ethically follow all the laws governing email marketing. They also have intimate knowledge of the inner workings of spam filters to reduce the chances of your emails getting canned.

PUTTING IT ALL TOGETHER

So now that we've talked about getting your emails across the Internet, let's take a look at the elements of an effective marketing email.

I. A Campaign is Only as Good as Its List

The most important part of your email campaign starts with your email address list. Your address list is like a fish you just bought at the grocery store. If you let it go too long, it starts to stink. You want to keep your address list clean and fresh. How do you go about doing that? First, you need to manage your list from the very start.

The best method for procuring email addresses on your website is to employ a double opt-in process. This is a two-step process to collect the addresses that involves the contact filling out an online form on your website. Once the email address is collected, your website sends a follow-up email to the person asking them to click on a link in the email to confirm their contact information. There are a couple of reasons why this is the best strategy to collect emails on your website. First, it verifies the email was input by the contact without any typing errors. Second, it legitimizes an ongoing relationship with the person. It also reinforces their participation in receiving emails from you.

There are other means to procure emails depending on your business and customer base. Trade shows, community events and networking opportunities are several ways you can supplement your online leads. Keep in mind, these contacts are probably not as invested in you or your business as much as someone who takes the time to fill out your contact form on your website.

Once your list is compiled, keep it up to date. You'll want to pay close attention to several measurements after you send out an email campaign. Check to see how many people haven't opened your email after a certain amount of time, say 30 or 45 days. Take those addresses out of future emails but keep them in case you want to invite them back at a later date. You'll also want to keep tabs on emails that bounce, that is, are undeliverable. There can be several reasons why the server was unable to deliver your email to the recipient. The person's inbox capacity may have been full, or the email address is no longer in use. Again, take these emails out of your active list.

II. Create a Scintillating Subject Line

De-spammed? Check. Clean address list? Check. So now you've got to get the recipients to open the email. You'll first need to consider how long to make the subject. Keep your subject heading short and sweet so the whole thing is visible in the inbox. I'd recommend around 50-60 characters. Good subject lines take some time and thought but can lead to a higher open rate. Some of the best subject lines can include some of the following information targeted for recipients:

- How the information benefits them
- Asking or answering questions
- Lists such as "3 Ways to Improve Open Rates"

Email marketing, like all marketing, is a work in progress. One question up for debate is how personalized you should make your emails. Should the subject line and email speak to the recipient by name or should it be more general. With traditional direct mail, studies have shown that using a person's name on the envelope and in the salutation of the letter are more effective than generic openings. So, if you have a credit card through your bank, they would send you a home equity loan solicitation addressed directly to you. The e-newsletter service MailChimp suggests that personalizing marketing emails improves open rates.

However, a study done by Temple University's Fox School of Business found that 95 percent of recipients of email marketing responded negatively when addressed by name in the email.

In my experience I haven't seen personalization affect open rates one way or the other. I strongly believe personalization depends on your relationship with the people on your list. For example, if you belong to a fitness center, it would probably address you differently than your financial advisor would.

One of my best email campaigns had the subject heading of "Hey!" That was it. But that underscores the relationship I have with the people on my list. They're familiar with the conversational tone in my emails, so seeing my name and the "Hey" was enough to get them to open my email. Keep in mind, I've built that relationship over years. It's not how you would want to address your contacts in your first email to them.

But don't take my word for it. Test it yourself and see if personalization clicks with your readers. Whichever way you decide to go, email marketing is flexible enough to accommodate different preferences. It makes it easy to personalize both the subject line and content if you choose to.

III. Create Inspiring Content

OK, you've finally gotten your contact to open your email. The clock is ticking. Studies show you have 15-20 seconds to get your message across before the person moves on to the next email. Make the next step crystal clear for them. Do you want them to attend a free webinar, visit your store, or save 10 percent if they place an order today?

With that amount of time, you'll want to have shorter copy with graphics that reinforce your message. Keep in mind, though, pictures sometimes get filtered out of messages, so make sure your copy can sell the offer on its own. Put your offer at the top of the email so your contacts won't have to scroll to see what you're selling. Also, when speaking to your customers, use "you." Who will benefit from this offer? You will, that's who.

Try not to clutter your email with too many offers. A good rule of thumb is one offer, many links. Give the reader multiple ways to reach your intended destination using both text and graphics.

IV. When to Send It

There isn't one best or worst time to send emails, although weekdays tend to do better than weekends. There's also some data that suggests the best time of day to send emails is around 10 a.m., but it's not significantly better than other times of day.

I've found that it all depends on your business, your market, and what you're trying to accomplish. The beauty of email marketing is you have the analytics available that show you when your recipients opened your emails, so you can easily determine the day and time that's best for your contacts.

FULFILLMENT AND FOLLOW-UP

Congratulations. You've successfully launched your email campaign. You now need to follow through on your offer and review your data. It's time to send out your e-book or ship out customer orders. You also want to give some thought to how you can grow your relationship. For example, let's say you do online marketing for a seed company. You have a customer who bought several packets of tomato seeds. You've set up your system to send out an email offer for herb seeds to anyone who buys tomato seeds. After all, nobody eats a tomato by itself.

It's also time to perform your after-action review. Among other things, your email analytics will be able to tell you:

- How many people opened the email
- When they opened the email
- How many people clicked on a link

Based on these analytics and your call-to-action responses, you'll be able to calculate your ROI to measure the success of your campaign.

EMAIL – STILL GOING STRONG

Whether your email marketing campaign is geared toward sales, downloads, or just informational, you'll find that a well-designed campaign that includes an up-to-date list, an eye-catching subject, killer content, and a clear call-to-action will produce positive results for your company. No matter what the "experts" say, email marketing is still going strong and will continue to be an important tool in the marketer's utility belt.

About Lindsay

Lindsay Dicks helps her clients tell their stories in the online world. Being brought up around a family of marketers, but a product of Generation Y, Lindsay naturally gravitated to the new world of on-line marketing. Lindsay began freelance writing in 2000 and soon after launched her own PR firm that thrived by offering an in-your-face "Guaranteed PR" that was one of the first of its type in the nation.

Lindsay's new media career is centered on her philosophy that "people buy people." Her goal is to help her clients build a relationship with their prospects and customers. Once that relationship is built and they learn to trust them as the expert in their field, then they will do business with them. Lindsay also built a proprietary process that utilizes social media marketing, content marketing and search engine optimization to create online "buzz" for her clients that helps them to convey their business and personal story. Lindsay's clientele spans the entire business map and ranges from doctors and small business owners to Inc. 500 CEOs.

Lindsay is a graduate of the University of Florida. She is the CEO of CelebritySites™, an online marketing company specializing in social media and online personal branding. Lindsay is recognized as one of the top online marketing experts in the world and has co-authored more than 25 best-selling books alongside authors such as Steve Forbes, Richard Branson, Brian Tracy, Jack Canfield (creator of the *Chicken Soup for the Soul* series), Dan Kennedy, Robert Allen, Dr. Ivan Misner (founder of BNI), Jay Conrad Levinson (author of the *Guerilla Marketing* series), Leigh Steinberg and many others, including the breakthrough hit *Celebrity Branding You!*

She has also been selected as one of America's PremierExperts™ and has been quoted in *Forbes, Newsweek, The Wall Street Journal, USA Today,* and *Inc. Magazine* as well as featured on NBC, ABC, and CBS television affiliates speaking on social media, search engine optimization and making more money online. Lindsay was also recently brought on FOX 35 News as their Online Marketing Expert.

Lindsay, a national speaker, has shared the stage with some of the top speakers in the world, including Brian Tracy, Lee Milteer, Ron LeGrand,

Arielle Ford, Leigh Steinberg, Dr. Nido Qubein, Dan Sullivan, David Bullock, Peter Shankman and many others. Lindsay was also a Producer on the Emmy-winning film, *Jacob's Turn*, and sits on the advisory board for the Global Economic Initiative.

You can connect with Lindsay at:

- Lindsay@CelebritySites.com
- www.twitter.com/LindsayMDicks
- www.facebook.com/LindsayDicks

CHAPTER 16

THE IMPACT OF CONNECTION

BY JW DICKS AND NICK NANTON

The scientist wanted a seat at the table.

The national conversations of the day all seemed to revolve about TV shows, movies, music, sports and other disposable entertainment. To him, people were losing sight of scientific facts and how they affected us all in profound ways, because the trivial had eclipsed the eternal. Even politics had become more like professional wrestling than actual serious discussions of serious issues.

Most academics thought it beneath themselves to participate in this kind of trivial pop culture world, so they pushed themselves away from the table. Carl Sagan, the astrophysicist, author and host of the original *Cosmos* who became famous partly for the way he enunciated "Billions and billions," used ancient history and highbrow literature as his reference points. Even though Sagan regularly appeared on *The Tonight Show with Johnny Carson*, Carson kept the dialogue intellectual and cultured—plus, he shared Sagan's interest in space and the universe. There wasn't much pandering to the crowd. But this scientist was different. He didn't exactly want to pander either. But he did want to *connect*. And to do that, he was willing to venture into pop culture territory.

And that's how one of the most popular directors of all time ended up feeling obligated to reshoot a scene in one of the hugest movie blockbusters of all time.

When the scientist saw James Cameron's *Titanic*, he saw a problem that nobody else noted. When Rose, played by Kate Winslet, was floating on the ocean under the night sky near the end of the movie, the scientist noticed that the stars were not in the proper positions for that time of year and that location. He emailed Cameron—and Cameron took his concern serious enough to redo the special effects on the constellations.

Then there was *The Daily Show with Jon Stewart*. The scientist was a regular guest and each time he was on, he would point out to Stewart that the animated globes in the show's open were spinning in the wrong direction. Finally, because of his hectoring, the show actually redid the open, so planet Earth was once again rotating correctly.

In 2013, his pop culture fact-checking hit its zenith when *Gravity*, starring Sandra Bullock and George Clooney, became a big box-office success. The space-based sci-fi drama was suddenly the object of a series of light-hearted tweets from the scientist, correcting various scientific goofs that were in the film, such as satellites generally circle the globe west to east, yet in the movie all the debris was moving east to west. Then there was the fact that Sandra Bullock's hair remained unruffled in zero-gravity conditions.

Suddenly, the scientist's tweeted corrections were being covered on national newscasts and spoofed on *Saturday Night Live*. He found himself front and center in the pop culture spotlight and, the next year, he ended up hosting a modern version of Carl Sagan's *Cosmos*, produced by *Family Guy* creator Seth McFarland. And the following year, he began hosting *StarTalk*, his own interview show, on the National Geographic channel.

Neil deGrasse Tyson had finally achieved his ambition of gaining a seat at the table.

Today's MediaMasters, those who know how to create a multi-platform presence with true impact, ignore trends and pop culture at their own peril. If you don't make an effort to connect with what's topical and "hot," you risk missing out on grabbing a substantial portion of your intended audience. Tyson understood this and made the calculation that he could spread his scientific message if he dove down into the pit of pop culture instead of acting like he was above it. In Tyson's own words:

"I kept people's attentions for longer if I plugged pop culture into what I was talking about. There's a lot of really great science for science's sake. But that gets people who already lean toward science. That gets the subset of people, not the majority. So, what I've been doing is attaching science to what you already care about...You come for the pop culture and stay for the science." [1]

And Tyson isn't the only MediaMaster who's dipped his toes in the pop culture water. One of our greatest MediaMasters of all time, Tony Robbins, has portrayed himself numerous times in sitcoms such as *Roseanne* and in movies such as *Men in Black* and *Shallow Hal*, starring Jack Black and Gwyneth Paltrow (where Robbins actually had a pivotal role, based on the screenwriter's real experience being coached by Robbins' courses). [2]

---

1. Eichel, Molly. "Neil deGrasse Tyson wants to talk to you about 'Star Wars' (and teach you some science)," *The Philadelphia Enquirer*, November 29, 2016. (http://www.philly.com/philly/entertainment/Neil-deGrasse-Tyson-movies.html)

2. Flanagan, Graham. "Tony Robbins Reveals the Real Story Behind his Unforgettable 'Shallow Hal' Cameo," *Business Insider*, March 28, 2015. (http://www.businessinsider.com/tony-robbins-shallow-hal-cameo-movie-jack-black-farrelly-brothers-2015-3)

What's key to Robbins' appearances is that, even when he's surrounded by silliness in the comedies just mentioned, his integrity remains intact. He generally portrays a life coach honestly interested in helping a character break through and make progress in their life. Both he and Tyson have been smart in their media strategy, in that they participate on their own terms, in ways that buttress their professional standing instead of tearing it down.

And that's just what you should be doing as an up and coming MediaMaster. In this chapter, we're going to discuss ways you too can connect with the culture around you and get your own seat at the mass media table—without surrendering your dignity.

Connection and The Power of Pop Culture

You sit down with a group of people who are total strangers. They begin talking amongst themselves and you sit patiently, wondering how to interact with them. Then they begin talking about something you actually know a lot about.

Suddenly, you have an opening. Suddenly, you can contribute, so you go ahead and comment on the conversation. And suddenly, you find you've established a connection with the others.

What we've just described is a process that, as a MediaMaster, should be your number one priority—to find common ground with every potential follower out there in the world and to leverage that common ground to your advantage.

Pop culture provides that common ground.

Just take a look at the top ten Twitter accounts, as of the moment we're writing this chapter. All of which have anywhere from 60 to 100 million followers, and are pop singers—Katy Perry, Rhianna, Justin Bieber, Taylor Swift, etc., six in all. The rest?

Comedian Ellen DeGeneres, the Twitter accounts of YouTube and Twitter, and former President Barack Obama.

Now maybe you don't know who any of those singers are. But maybe you should. And someone else you should check out is none other than Neil deGrasse Tyson, who once told an audience of physicists, scientists, and science students, "If you ever need to communicate with anyone who isn't a physicist, go learn who these people are. Because everybody else knows who they are. Otherwise don't go home crying that nobody understands you. You testify to Congress and you say they don't get it, there's something wrong with them. Noooooo. There's something missing in your lexicon because everybody else is fluent here. And if you want them to fund what you're doing, learn something about what people are doing outside of the laboratory."[3]

Take the above paragraph and replace the references to scientists with references to your own area of expertise and you'll see how Tyson's advice applies to your MediaMastery. When you only focus on what you do, you're just playing in your own pond, but there's a whole wide ocean of people out there you're not connecting with. And that's not the kind of mindset that's going to take you places.

We understand that concept, which is why we've created content that has referenced Kim Kardashian, Seinfeld, Marvel Superheroes and at least two of the singers represented on that top ten Twitter list (Justins Timberlake and Bieber, if you must know!).

Here's why it's important to utilize pop culture at least occasionally. There may be someone out there who would love your stuff. Who would eat up everything you say and write. But that someone

---

3. Calla Cofield, "Neil deGrasse Tyson on Science in Popular Culture," APS News, May 2015. (https://www.aps.org/publications/apsnews/201405/tyson.cfm)

might have no idea of who you are or what you're all about. So, obviously, they're not going to seek you out, because, well, why should they? *They don't know enough about you or your subject matter.*

However, you can provide an entry point that will draw them in if you utilize subject matter that is familiar to them to make a point. And that entry point is pop culture.

Pop culture has always been with us, of course, in one form or another. But today, it's much more a part of everyone's lives with the explosion of popularity of social media. That creates a gigantic opportunity for any MediaMaster to connect with new audiences. By utilizing popular celebrities, movies, TV shows and songs in content and posts, you will automatically capture the interest of someone who might have never given you another look.

This can be essential to your ongoing success. There will come a time when you plateau in terms of the numbers of your followers. You may have exhausted your own circles of influence as well as those who might be directly interested in your message. That's when it's critical to build your powers of connection with the public at large. And keying into the latest big thing in pop culture, as well as hot new trends and evergreen greats, can be an amazing way to capture a whole new crowd.

You want more proof? Consider that the #1 car brand in America, Ford, is also the #1 company to practice product placement— they've paid to place their vehicles in over a hundred Hollywood blockbusters in recent years. Why? So their cars and trucks can become an integral part of the biggest pop culture hits out there. The #2 company for product placement? Apple. No slouch either.

As one marketing expert puts it, "In terms of reaching a wide audience, nothing compares to popular culture marketing. Pop culture has never been so widely transmitted as it is today, and consumers are far more receptive to public fascinations due to the ubiquity of social media and the Internet. With more pop culture content than ever before, brands are taking advantage of fads and leveraging particular celebrities and cultural phenomena to market products and services."[4]

Why shouldn't your MediaMaster brand take advantage too?

HOW TO MAKE YOUR CONTENT POP

If you're wondering how exactly to put pop culture to work for you, here are a few simple strategies that are very effective when your aim is to gain your content more looks and more "likes."

- **A Star Shares Your Passion**
  Gwyneth Paltrow is famous not only for her acting, but also for her lifestyle products. Jay Leno? The former number one late night talk show host now has a whole show about cars, a hobby he shares with fellow funnyman Jerry Seinfeld. And Seth McFarland's interest for science is what prompted him to back Neil deGrasse Tyson's *Cosmos* series, as detailed earlier. The point is, there are a host of celebrities out there who are known not only for their entertainment skills, but also their other outside interests that they enjoy talking about and sharing with the public. When an A-list star has a passion that dovetails with your MediaMaster brand, use them in your content and promote that content with the star's name. You'll find their fans flocking to your posts.

- **A Blockbuster Needs to Be Busted**
  Let's say you're a lawyer and a movie or a TV show depicting a legal case turns out to be a smash. What's your take on what you saw? Did the writers nail the legal aspects correctly, or did they fudge the facts to make a more entertaining yarn?

---

4. Scharf, Courtney, "How Companies Have Used Popular Culture Marketing to Increase Brand Exposure," *Trendhunter.com*, November 6, 2012. (http://www.trendreports.com/article/popular-culture-marketing)

Just as Tyson took on *Gravity* and made a public splash, you too can critique a series or film that centers around your expertise—and evaluate its accuracy. You'll not only attract viewers of the show or film, you'll also impress them with your knowledge and experience.

- **If the Fad Fits…**
Certain crazes catch on fire with the public and make their presence known throughout Facebook and Twitter, not to mention other social media platforms. Not too long ago, the mobile game Pokémon GO had players walking into rivers and falling off cliffs, in search of elusive (and nonexistent!) Pokémon characters. Many savvy brick-and-mortar businesses actually used the presence of a virtual Pokémon within their walls to promote themselves. Then there was the "ice bucket" challenge in which people dumped ice water over their heads in order to help fight the crippling disease, ALS. Well, of course, many celebrities and MediaMasters saw the advantage in not only promoting a worthy cause, but also boosting their profile—so they too dumped buckets of ice water over their heads to make a social media splash.

Whatever the latest gone-viral fad might be, there is probably a way to utilize it to your advantage. For example, right now, fidget spinners, a toy meant to relieve stress and anxiety, are huge. If you're a MediaMaster who specializes in life coaching, the fidget spinner just might be the perfect opening for you to discuss dealing with normal life tensions.

- **Songs that Suit Your Soundtrack**
Before many a MediaMaster speaking engagement, you'll most likely hear a specific set of songs designed to amplify that MediaMaster's message as well as excite the crowd. The more contemporary and popular the music, the more it resonates with a public that loves to rock out. So choose current songs that fit in with your brand and see if they not

only work for your live talks, but also in your content. For example, break down the lyrics of a smash hit that reflects your approach in a blog post and analyze why it resonates with so many people.

- **Try on a Template**
  Often, you can build an entire book or series of videos around a pop culture concept that will lift it above your competition. For example, you'll currently find a score of marketing and MediaMaster books centered around a superhero theme, because movies like *The Avengers* and *Justice League* are the biggest film events in the world these days. You can also find a host of content with themes that reflect *Star Wars* movies, the *Game of Thrones* series, and even philosophy books based on *South Park*! With that in mind, look for a popular franchise that might appeal to your target audience and also can be connected to your messaging.

THE PERILS OF POP CULTURE

While the upside of pop culture references can be huge, the downside can also be a bit daunting. Here are a few danger zones you'll want to avoid when you're connecting through pop culture.

- **Steer Clear of Controversy**
  An ill-placed tweet by a star can sink his or her reputation in a flash—and if that's the celebrity you've pinned a post on, that reflects badly on you. So, avoid referencing personalities, as well as music and TV series, that are either known for or have the potential to create a negative media frenzy. Political figures in particular can land you in hot water, because you never know when they're going to attack (or be attacked) on subject matter you shouldn't be taking a public stand on. The result could be the splitting of the total audience that's available to you.

Of course, there are occasions when you can't predict this kind of trouble. In that case, the public usually can't either—so they'll accept a heartfelt apology from you and that will probably be the end of it.

- **Don't Be Too Late to the Party**
  You ever meet that guy who' s still doing Austin Powers jokes like it's 2002? Or doing a Borat accent like it's 2006? Don't ever be that guy. If you're going to hitch your wagon to a pop culture phenomenon, make sure it's not one that's past its expiration date. Not sure about one? Well, if you have kids, ask them and they'll be *very* quick to tell you how uncool you're being!

- **Embrace Evergreens**
  For the kinds of content that you want to stand the test of time—books, videos, etc.—avoid quick-to-burst pop culture bubbles that could seem hopelessly outdated the minute you release your material. For example, ephemeral film hits and reality shows that are very "of the moment" (we're looking at you, *Jersey Shore*) will be quickly forgotten—while icons like *Batman* and *Star Wars* will undoubtedly be here for the long run.

- **Don't Force a Fit**
  Don't get us wrong, there are a lot of weird and wonderful ways to make pop culture references work, even when they shouldn't. But it's painful to see someone awkwardly attach say, the current teen music idol to their business selling annuities when one really does have nothing to do with the other. Again, there might be a fun way to make it work—and if you find that way, go for it—but if you're just using a famous name or title for the sake of using it, and you haven't really found a way to organically connect it to your content, it will read as totally uncool. Again…ask your kids! (Or, if you don't have any, ask a neighbor's!)

As we've discussed, pop culture can be a heavy-duty weapon in your ongoing battle to engage eyeballs and amass followers. It provides a recognizable and fun entry point for someone who may have no idea of who you are to sample what you have to say—and hopefully return for more. As noted, common ground is crucial to starting a vibrant conversation, and that's where leveraging pop culture can really make an impact.

We began this chapter by talking about how Neil deGrasse Tyson used popular movies like *Titanic* and *Gravity* to make his impact. Let's end with another one of his amazing examples of how a specific expertise can take an everyday pop culture moment and transform it into an unbelievable branding opportunity for a MediaMaster.

One day, Tyson was waiting for a television show taping to begin, so he had a half-hour to kill. He began randomly channel-surfing to occupy the time. He happened upon a football game going on between the Cincinnati Bengals and the Seattle Seahawks, a game which had just gone into overtime after four quarters of play ended up in a tie score. Well, Tyson decided to see how the game came out, as it would fill up his 30 minutes nicely—and the Bengals pulled it out with a barely-successful field goal kick. Tyson watched carefully as the football hit the left upright, and then flew in between the goalposts for the win.

That would have been it for most viewers. But not Tyson. He did some quick calculations on his phone and then tweeted the following:

"Today's @Bengals winning OT field goal was likely enabled by a 1/3-in deflection to the right, caused by Earth's Rotation."

The tweet ended up garnering almost five million "likes" and was mentioned by the sportscasters doing the game. It was also reported on the evening news. And here's Tyson breaking down why the tweet had such impact:

"…if you think about that tweet, I didn't have to explain what

167

football is. I didn't have to explain what a field goal is or that it's worth three points or that their game was happening at all. I didn't have to remind you what these teams are. There's a large enough pop culture sector that cares so much about football that if you learn that the rotation of the earth influenced a football, you are all over that piece of information."[5]

The common ground of pop culture creates connection with impact—and isn't that what every MediaMaster loves to see happen in today's New Economy?

5. Miller, Liz Shannon. "Why Neil deGrasse Tyson Loves Spreading Science With Pop Culture," *Indiewire.com*, August 15th, 2016. (http://www.indiewire.com/2016/08/neil-degrasse-tyson-interview-cosmos-gravity-falls-startalk-emmys-1201717034/)

About JW

JW Dicks, Esq., is a *Wall Street Journal* Best-Selling Author®, Emmy Award-Winning Producer, publisher, board member, and co-founder of organizations such as The National Academy of Best-Selling Authors® and The National Association of Experts, Writers and Speakers®.

JW is the CEO of DNAgency and is a strategic business development consultant to both domestic and international clients. He has been quoted on business and financial topics in national media such as *USA Today, The Wall Street Journal, Newsweek, Forbes, CNBC.com*, and *Fortune Magazine Small Business.*

Considered a thought leader and curator of information, JW has more than forty-three published business and legal books to his credit and has co-authored with legends like Jack Canfield, Brian Tracy, Tom Hopkins, Dr. Nido Qubein, Dr. Ivan Misner, Dan Kennedy, and Mari Smith. He is the Editor and Publisher of *ThoughtLeader® Magazine.*

JW is called the "Expert to the Experts" and has appeared on business television shows airing on ABC, NBC, CBS, and FOX affiliates around the country and co-produces and syndicates a line of franchised business television shows such as *Success Today, Wall Street Today, Hollywood Live*, and *Profiles of Success*. He has received an Emmy® Award as Executive Producer of the film, *Mi Casa Hogar.*

JW and his wife of forty-three years, Linda, have two daughters, three granddaughters, and two Yorkies. He is a sixth-generation Floridian and splits his time between his home in Orlando and his beach house on Florida's west coast.

About Nick

An Emmy Award-Winning Director and Producer, Nick Nanton, Esq., produces media and branded content for top thought leaders and media personalities around the world. Recognized as a leading expert on branding and storytelling, Nick has authored more than two dozen Best-Selling books (including *The Wall Street Journal* Best-Seller, *StorySelling*™) and produced and directed more than 40 documentaries, earning 5 Emmy Awards and 14 nominations. Nick speaks to audiences internationally on the topics of branding, entertainment, media, business and storytelling at major universities and events.

As the CEO of DNA Media, Nick oversees a portfolio of companies including: The Dicks + Nanton Agency (an international agency with more than 3000 clients in 36 countries), Dicks + Nanton Productions, Ambitious.com, CelebrityPress, DNA Films®, DNA Pulse, and DNA Capital Ventures. Nick is an award-winning director, producer and songwriter who has worked on everything from large-scale events to television shows with the likes of Steve Forbes, Ivanka Trump, Sir Richard Branson, Rudy Ruettiger (inspiration for the Hollywood blockbuster, *RUDY*), Jack Canfield (*The Secret*, creator of the *Chicken Soup for the Soul* Series), Brian Tracy, Michael E. Gerber, Tom Hopkins, Dan Kennedy and many more.

Nick has been seen in *USA Today, The Wall Street Journal, Newsweek, BusinessWeek, Inc. Magazine, The New York Times, Entrepreneur® Magazine, Forbes*, and *FastCompany*. He has appeared on ABC, NBC, CBS, and FOX television affiliates across the country as well as on CNN, FOX News, CNBC, and MSNBC from coast to coast.

Nick is a member of the Florida Bar, a voting member of The National Academy of Recording Arts & Sciences (Home to the GRAMMYs), a member of The National Academy of Television Arts & Sciences (Home to the EMMYs), co-founder of The National Academy of Best-Selling Authors®, and serves on the Innovation Board of the XPRIZE Foundation, a non-profit organization dedicated to bringing about "radical breakthroughs for the benefit of humanity" through incentivized competition – best known for its Ansari XPRIZE which incentivized the first private space flight and was the catalyst for Richard Branson's Virgin Galactic.

Nick also enjoys serving as an Elder at Orangewood Church, working with Young Life, Downtown Credo Orlando, Entrepreneurs International and rooting for the Florida Gators with his wife Kristina and their three children, Brock, Bowen and Addison.

Learn more at:

- www.NickNanton.com
- www.CelebrityBrandingAgency.com

CHAPTER 17

THE NEVER-ENDING REFERRAL SYSTEM

BY GREG ROLLETT

It was a Friday night. One of the rare nights when we left the house and left the two kids at home. With a two-year old and a six-month-old, it has become increasingly harder to have a Friday night with friends.

This was a nice exception.

My mother-in-law had come over and was watching the little guys so Jen and I could have an evening out.

- When you haven't had a date night in months (maybe a year), where do you go?
- When you have one shot to pick the right restaurant, with thousands to choose from, who gets the business?

1. There's Facebook. You can create a post and ask your friends for recommendations.

2. There's Yelp.

3. There's Google.

4. There is the good old fashioned drive-by.

5. You can call or text your close circle.

In each of the options we are looking for a referral. We are looking for a source that we trust to give us a recommendation of where to spend our night on the town.

With things like restaurants and movies, people are quick to tell you what they loved and what they hated.

- *"Go see that movie right now."*
- *"Don't waste your money."*
- *"You have to check out this new restaurant."*

This might seem trivial, but when you understand why we make recommendations for restaurants, bars, vacation destinations and what movies to see, you can start to understand what you need to do in order to get your clients to start referring you.

We all want more referrals. Many times these are our best clients. They contact you and are already half-way through the door. All you generally have to do is "not mess it up."

WHY DOES THIS HAPPEN?

Because someone that they trust told them they have to use you. With this trust, they had help making up their mind, before you ever had an opportunity to open your mouth and go through your presentation.

Knowing that you want more referrals and actually getting them is a completely different story. *Referrals don't just happen.* They are not automatic just because you delivered a great service or experience.

Referrals happen because they are engineered. Businesses get the most referrals when they have a system to generate them. They do not leave it up to chance. In fact, they make their referral system a priority, just as you might have made lead generation a priority.

The businesses that get the most referrals build their referral system with the same money, time, resources and attention that they would anything else in their business.

The majority of business owners hope that their great service is enough to get their clients talking about them. This might produce a referral here or there. Here or there is not how you want to run your business. You want to play at an elite level and to do so, you must put together a referral system. I am going to walk you through the referral system that we have been implementing for our clients to generate a stream of never-ending referrals.

Never-ending means that your current clients will be trained and conditioned to send you referrals. The newly-referred clients will then also be conditioned to refer you new clients as that is how they were introduced to you. Once this system is in place, the chain never breaks and you will develop never-ending referrals.

So, how do you create this Never-Ending Referral System?

You begin to create your Never-Ending Referral System by understanding how referrals take place and the psychology of a referral. My friend and marketing expert Dean Jackson, from the iLoveMarketing Podcast, explained to me on an episode of *Celebrity Expert Live* that three things must align for a referral to take place.

Those three things are:
1. The person referring has to notice that the conversation is about what you do.
2. They then have to think about you.
3. They have to introduce you to the conversation.

If those three conditions are not met, you have lost the battle before it even begins. The good news is that you can help to manufacture the referral process by using the Never-Ending Referral System I am about to unveil to you.

When you follow the simple steps outlined below, you will start to pop up in general conversations and enter the mind of your clients exactly when you want them to think of you. You will be showing up in their life like a happily invited guest, delivering value and goodwill that will transfer to the social situations your clients enter in their daily lives. Your clients will want to bring your name up in conversation and talk about the value you bring to your life. This can only happen when you show up in their lives – when you make a conscious decision to appear in their lives more often.

Many business owners stop showing up after the initial transaction. Doing this will make your client forget you in a heartbeat. When you stop showing up and adding massive value to the lives of your clients, someone else will. They will become distracted and then engage with other products or services that are playing a role in their lives.

This doesn't have to mean competition either. If you are a financial advisor and you just signed a client up for one of your retirement programs, what are you doing to continue the relationship after the deal is signed? Did you mail them a new client gift or welcome package? Are you talking to them regularly or only at their annual portfolio review?

A lot can happen in that year. When you stop paying attention to your clients, they stop paying attention to you. With the busy lives we lead they might even forget your name. But not if you use the system I am about to reveal to you.

On the flip-side, if you are showing up in their lives on a regular basis with great tips, resources, education and entertainment, your clients are thinking about you, and their subconscious mind will be trained to bring you up in conversation.

When you up the ante and start to become "brag material" you will get mentioned more and more. By "brag material" I mean that you are such an important asset in their lives that they want to bring you up, and what you have done for them to brag to their friends. This gives them a social advantage over their friends.

Think about it like keeping up with the Joneses. The easy brags are about the new toys they have purchased, like the newest iPhone or tablet. Things like vacations they went on or cars they have upgraded to. I want you to think about how to enter their lives at this level. I will explain how we help our clients to do this momentarily.

Finally, I want you to create every asset in your marketing arsenal to have pass-on value. I want your clients to love "your stuff" so much that they are happy to pass it on to a friend. This makes the referral-asking process easy, fun and actionable. Look, no one wants to be asked to write down a list of names of people that you might be able to help. It makes they feel uncomfortable and uneasy. This is a major turn-off, especially the higher you climb on the wealth and affluence ladder.

Instead, you want to make it easy for your clients to refer you by giving them things to pass on, like a copy of your book or a newsletter filled with great content and resources. I'll talk more about this in a minute. So now you know what this system looks like and what it can do for your business, it's time to get into the nuts and bolts of the Never-Ending Referral System and lay it out for you to copy in your own business. Let's get to it.

THE THREE STEPS TO CREATING A NEVER-ENDING REFERRAL SYSTEM

The three steps outlined below require you to put in some effort to create something worthy for your clients going out into the world and talking about you.

I can assure you that spending the time to create these assets and systems will be worth every moment spent putting them together. Remember, the goal is to build an army of clients who are excited about working with you, so much so that they expect you to send them items of massive goodwill and in turn, will go out to their social circles and brag about how great you are.

Are you ready? Good, let's go.

Step 1: Send every Client (and every prospect) a Personality-Driven Newsletter in the Mail

There is no replacement for a physical print newsletter that you mail to your clients each and every month. In attempts to cut costs or to leverage technology, like email, so many business owners have gotten away from sending a print newsletter in lieu of an email newsletter. Trust me when I tell you - this is a terrible mistake to make in your business.

Writing up a personal letter, printing it and putting a stamp on it is powerful. It says you care. It says, *"this is something worth reading."* It is also a monthly reminder of who you are, what you do and what you are doing. This is an important piece to remember. Even if you only meet with your clients once or twice a year, sending the newsletter in the mail every month reminds them that you exist, that you are out there working for them and acts like a quick meeting over coffee you are having with a client.

Print newsletters are the biggest asset we have in our business and the business of every client we get to work with. The mistake most entrepreneurs make with newsletters is making them boring. They make their newsletter read like something that was slapped together because it had to get out.

You on the other hand are developing a Never-Ending Referral

System. That means your newsletter content needs to be something worth talking about. Your newsletter needs to have content that is worth sharing, talking about and worthy of being discussed in a conversation.

This only happens when you inject your personality into it. You have to open up and talk about your life, your clients, issues and matters that mean something to you and sharing real opinions that are heartfelt and sincere.

The newsletters we create for our clients come right from the mouth of our experts. We get experts and entrepreneurs to open up about their vacations, their pets, their favorite sports teams, conversations they are having with their clients and things that are boiling in their skin. The content this turns into has passion. It has life. It lets your clients into your life. And in turn you begin to have a real relationship with them that goes way beyond just the product you sold them or the service you are providing.

After you create your print newsletter and start sending it out monthly, you then start sending your clients and top prospects...

Step 2: The Monthly Item of Value

The newsletter is my favorite marketing item to get into the hands of your clients on a monthly basis. As great as the newsletter is, it only shows up once a month. I want to consume the lives of my clients and help them as much as possible. That's where a monthly item of value comes into the picture.

For our financial advisors in our Ambitious Advisor Program, we write, design and send out a printed special report each and every single month that gets customized and sent to the clients of our advisors. The advisors in the program love this, as it allows them to put something that has extreme value into the hands of their clients that can easily be passed onto a friend to stimulate referrals.

One of our advisors told us about an older woman who was a client, but was very quiet. She was a good client, but sent over referrals or participated in client events. Then she began receiving these monthly special reports. Immediately she saw the value in the reports and began sharing them with neighbors. She finally felt she "had something" to share with her neighbors and brag about her advisor.

She may have never sent a referral over in her entire life had this advisor not spent the few dollars a month to print and ship her this item of value. Now she has someone on the front lines talking about his services for him, pre-conditioning referrals to get excited to work with him.

This monthly item of value doesn't have to be a special report.

- It can be a CD of a recording where you interview another expert or showcase a client that can add value to their lives.

- It can be a few newspaper or magazine articles you cut out and sent along with a note. This positions you as a curator of content and someone who has their ear to the street. This makes it easy for someone to bring your name up in conversation when someone has a question and needs to find a resource that has the answer.

- This monthly item of value can be videos that you shoot and email out to your clients, but are only seen by clients. It could be deals and offers from those you have relationships with.

- No matter what your monthly item of value, you must create something that excites and motivates your clients. And you must do it frequently so you are constantly appearing in their lives.

And if you just do the first two steps you are now showing up two times every month. That is 24 times in one year. What would that do for your business and your referrals? If you are doing nothing right now, it's 24X more effective. But when you couple this with Step 3, your stock and goodwill with your clients will go through the roof!

<u>Step 3:</u> The "I'm Thinking About You" Package

Now it's time to take your Never-Ending Referral System to a whole 'nother level. When you start to add Step 3 to your referral marketing, your business will never be the same.

At this level, you are at the forefront of the minds of your clients every time you need to be. At Step 3 you start to get your clients to brag about their relationship with you. The great news is that this step is not difficult, but requires some planning, some time and some attention.

In Step 3 you are going to create events, packages and items that your clients would have only ever received from their close friends and family members. They would never imagine that you would be thinking of them like this. And that is where you begin to win and see your business rise to an elite level.

So what can you send to your clients to make them stop in their tracks and put you at the top of their conscious mind? You can start by hosting events for your clients. These cannot be "regular events." These needs to be events that their friends could never get invited to.

This might be a wine tasting at a private club or vineyard. This might be box seats to a sporting event. It may be the opening of an art gallery. It may be listening to a speaker that you have special access to. The event has to be special. It has to be something your clients want to go to and not feel like they are going out of obligation.

For some clients we have put together movie screenings where your clients would get to see a new movie the day before the rest of the world. The entry fee, bring a friend.

To pull this off you need to send invitations, make the event feel exclusive and make it a truly big deal. You want your clients to talk to their friends before and after the event, about how you are thinking of them and giving them experiences that they could never imagine pulling off themselves.

But you don't need to throw an event to create the "I'm thinking of you" feeling. You could just host a contest with incredible prizes. We have helped our clients to throw contests like an annual March Madness Bracket competition with big prizes that included a cruise for two, spa retreats and more.

We then include their social circle, by mailing tickets that look like NCAA game tickets to pass out to their friends. The incentive, if their friend that was referred in wins the competition, the client would also receive a prize. These contests are a fun way to bring in a lot of referrals fast, and also show these referrals how much fun your company is, once you become part of the family.

After contests, you can find timely gifts and packages to send to your clients based on holidays, events and pop culture. For Veteran's Day, we created a campaign for financial advisors to mail a copy of *Saving Private Ryan* to their clients where they could invite their friends over to watch the film. Even if they don't invite the friends over to watch, they still have something to talk about the next time everyone gets together. That is a big win.

We have sent out stuffed groundhogs with the logo of our clients on the groundhog's t-shirt, making reference to waking up every day like the last day and if you know anyone waking up like Bill Murray to give them this groundhog.

These gifts are not expensive and go a long way towards building your business with a staple of never-ending referrals.

PUTTING YOUR NEVER-ENDING REFERRAL SYSTEM INTO ACTION

You now have the blueprint to create never-ending referrals. As I mentioned at the onset, this is a system that requires some work and some time. However, once you get everything up and running, it becomes a machine... a SYSTEM.

You begin to know your ROI like any other marketing channel and will be able to make decisions based on real returns. *No matter where you start, the thing to do now is to get started.* Start with the newsletter. Start with a monthly item of value.

Start becoming someone your clients look forward to hearing from and be a part of their lives. This will set you up with new business for as long as you want. Here's to creating your own Never-Ending Referral System.

About Greg

Greg Rollett is an Emmy® Award-Winning Producer, Best-Selling Author and Marketing Expert who works with experts, authors and entrepreneurs all over the world. He utilizes the power of new media, direct response and personality-driven marketing to attract more clients and to create more freedom in the businesses and lives of his clients.

After creating a successful string of his own educational products and businesses, Greg began helping others in the production and marketing of their own products and services.

Greg has written for *Mashable, Fast Company, Inc.com, the Huffington Post*, AOL, AMEX's *OPEN Forum* and others, and continues to share his message helping experts and entrepreneurs grow their business through marketing.

He has co-authored best-selling books with Jack Canfield, Dan Kennedy, Brian Tracy, Tom Hopkins, James Malinchak, Robert Allen, Ryan Lee and many other leading experts from around the world.

Greg's client list includes Michael Gerber, Brian Tracy, Tom Hopkins, Sally Hogshead, Coca-Cola, Miller Lite and Warner Brothers, along with thousands of entrepreneurs and small-business owners across the world. Greg's work has been featured on FOX News, ABC, NBC, CBS, CNN, *USA Today, Inc. Magazine, Fast Company, The Wall Street Journal, The Daily Buzz* and more.

To contact Greg, please visit:

- http://ambitious.com
- greg@ambitious.com